The tortellini experience
Adrian Benvenuto

Published by: Adrian Benvenuto

ISBN: 979-12-200-1828-9

2nd Edition May 2017

Copyright © 2017 by Adrian Benvenuto

All rights reserved. No part of this publication may be reproduced, distributed, or transmitted in any form or by any means, including photocopying, recording, or other electronic or mechanical methods, without the prior written permission of the publisher, except in the case of brief quotations embodied in critical reviews and certain other non-commercial uses permitted by copyright law. For permission requests, write to the publisher, at the email address below.

Adrian Benvenuto
Bologna, Italia
Email: info@ilbenvenuto-bologna.com

Author's Note

Benvenuto – Welcome!

I am a first generation Canadian, born and raised in Toronto by Italian parents who had departed Calabria Italy to immigrate to Canada. I always felt the urge to move to Italy, and in 2010, I made the move. Eventually, I ended-up in Bologna, where I started a Bed and Breakfast with my partner called **il Benvenuto Bologna** (www.ilbenvenuto-bologna.com). We have been open since September 2014, and this book shares my experiences of creating our B&B in Italy.

The book is organized in three main sections. The first section describes the journey of arriving in Italy and searching for the right place to run a B&B. The second explores the renovation process, and the third shares our experiences of running the B&B.

If you have ever considered starting a Bed and Breakfast in Italy, you will find real tips and advice, which we have learned from our successes, and of course from our errors.

The book is also an introduction to Bologna. Bologna is a city that offers vibrant Italian modern culture, in a medieval setting. As you read the stories, I hope that you too can discover the unique personality of this city that I have come to love.

The journey hasn't always been easy, and the stories provide honest insight into some of the challenges that I faced while trying to build a new life in a different country.

It's exciting to welcome you to this experience, and to our B&B, il Benvenuto Bologna!

Contents

1	**An Intro to Life Running a Bed & Breakfast**	**6**
1.1	A perfect storm of problems	7
2	**Searching for the Right Home for a B&B**	**18**
2.1	Wandering through the streets of Milano	19
2.2	The journey or the destination?	24
2.3	One second of fame in Italy	31
2.4	Bologna – a city of water?	36
2.5	Cosa facciamo stasera?	41
2.6	A needle in a haystack?	47
2.7	The Notaio	51
2.8	What did I get myself into?	56
2.9	My guilty pleasure	58
2.10	Let the demolition begin!	60
2.11	The break	65
3	**The Renovations**	**67**
3.1	Why should laws be logical?	68
3.2	Il Computo Metrico – your renovation bible	72
3.3	What - no spaghetti bolognese?	78
3.4	All in the name	81
3.5	A step back in time	87
3.6	Sound-proofing or dumb-proofing?	92
3.7	The scavenger hunt	96
3.8	Where did all the money go?	100
4	**Learning to Operate a Bed & Breakfast**	**103**
4.1	Where's the party?	104
4.2	Bologna the hidden	114
4.3	Circumventing the rules – a common Italian pastime	121
4.4	Don't forget the red tape	126

4.5	The two Sicilians	131
4.6	The case of the exploding shower-heads	136
4.7	The tortellini experience	138
4.8	You can't satisfy everyone	145
4.9	Comedy of errors	149
4.10	Non fare polemiche - Don't rock the boat	155
4.11	Kettle shrimps, anyone?	161
4.12	Navigating mortgages	165
4.13	Craving a great bolognese meal?	171
4.14	Sensitive egos...	176
4.15	A little visit from the city	184
4.16	The next chapter	189

5 Recipes   **191**

| 5.1 | Paola Pini's Tortellini in Brodo | 192 |

6 Endnotes   **206**

1 An Intro to Life Running a Bed & Breakfast

1.1
A perfect storm of problems

I've been reflecting, as I watch the scenery of the plain of the Po speed past at 300km an hour, on what's compelling me to write down my experiences as a Bed and Breakfast owner in Bologna, Italy.

Maybe I'm motivated to share my stories with people who might find them entertaining, or even inspiring, as a guest suggested this weekend after watching us trying to stay afloat from a perfect storm of problems.

This could also be my own brand of therapy, where I can sketch out a space to reflect on and digest my experiences over the last few years.

Or perhaps I'm launching my next challenge, and fulfilling an old romantic daydream of being an author. Why not write about what I've learned?

I'm not sure what type of author I'll become, if at all. However, as I read these first few sentences keyed into the notes app of my smart phone, which sound like they are trying hard to be profound and intellectual, I promise you that I won't take myself too seriously. After all, I'm a first generation Canadian of southern Italian immigrants, who has found my way back to the 'homeland', and has opened a Bed and Breakfast in Bologna - the home of tortellini, tagliatelle al ragù (don't make the mistake of calling it spaghetti bolognese), and some of the best cremerie (ice-cream parlours) that I have had the pleasure to savour.

I do also promise to keep this dialogue honest, and as engaging as possible!

Now, where to start. This first chapter describes the perfect storm of problems we experienced during the first weekend of February 2015.

While kind of a clichéd metaphor, a 'storm' is very fitting because it all started with an actual storm.

In most parts of Italy, outside of the mountain regions, a snow storm is a big event. The build-up before the storm is dramatic, with both news channels and friends advising of the upcoming peril. The actual storm is enchanting, as the view of snow covering the medieval palazzi (buildings) and statues in the piazze (town squares) is sublime and inspiring. The cleanup however, is a comedy of errors.

In Toronto, 30 centimetres of snow is a common winter snow-fall. In Bologna, it became the source of great drama. The local papers dubbed it "Big Snow" (and yes, they used the English words, as Italians love to adopt English terms). (Big Snow Bologna Article - Corriere di Bologna[1])

At first, we were amused. Facebook was full of postings from friends showing beautiful street sceneries painted in white. The view from our windows was entertaining, as we watched locals trying to remove the snow on their cars without snow/ice scrapers. There was even one person trying to protect her car windshield from the snowfall by placing a large piece of cardboard over it. I also held my breath watching an inexperienced tractor driver slowly ploughing the snow on our street, wondering if he was going to damage one of the parked cars or mopeds.

However, while observing the follies with a bit too much smugness, we gradually started to learn that we weren't prepared for the troubles that a snowfall can bring in Italy.

One couple, for whom we woke up at 4:30am to prepare breakfast and accommodate their early departure to the airport at 5:30am, ended up calling us from the airport because all the flights that morning were cancelled due to the snow. They were stuck in Bologna for two more days. Unfortunately, we were fully booked the following two nights and couldn't help them out.

While we normally call ahead to reserve a taxi for early morning departures, we've never called ahead for late morning or afternoon rides. Our next guests were scheduled to check-out later that morning, and needed a taxi to the airport. Starting to realise that it would be different that day, I began to call all the taxi companies and private chauffeur services. All I heard were busy signals for the next four hours. When I finally succeeded in reaching a representative from one private service, she explained, somewhat amused, that of course there were no cars available until at least late afternoon. Our guests were stuck taking the public bus to the airport.

> **Traveller Storm Tip:** Anticipate transportation difficulties with bad weather, and reserve you transport in advance. For those who think you are safe with your rental cars, ask yourself - will my car be ready when I need it? You might find your car blocked by a nice pile of snow left by the ploughs. Or better yet, did you park under a tree? Trees are rarely maintained regularly, and one storm can leave a splattering of branches on sidewalks, streets, and even on cars.

Up to this point, the events were more interesting, than stressful. At around 11:00 am, I had a couple of spare minutes and went to take a shower. I turned on the shower faucet, and waited for the hot water to arrive. I waited, and waited some more. I continued waiting for another minute until I eventually had to admit that there was no hot water! In some buildings, like ours, the hot water is heated centrally, and not by separate boilers in each apartment. That meant that if we didn't have hot water in our B&B, no one in the building had hot water. What's worse is that if the central boiler in the building is not heating the water needed in the apartments, it's also not heating the liquid used for the central heating system. Shit, there was no heat either!

Fortunately, the lack of heating in our B&B wasn't a problem. We invested in units for each room that could act as both air-conditioners and heaters. On the other hand, we never anticipated that the hot water boiler in the whole building could break down.

> **B&B Owner Tip:** Cost out options and consider investing in a back-up system to heat your water if your primary system fails. Naturally, travellers expect a hot shower to clean off a long day's travel. While it might have been expensive to set-up a backup system for each room, we realized that we could have created one spare bathroom with an independently heated shower, which could be used in emergencies. While too late now, maybe it's an idea for the next B&B ;-).

A sense of anxiety was settling in now, and some colourful language started to flow. We were expecting a full house of new arrivals that evening, and what would we do if the hot water could not be fixed in time? Would we need to start thinking of alternate hotel arrangements for our guests?

At this point, I grabbed my cell and dialled the office number of the Condo Administrator to report the problem. Ring, ring, ring....no answer. I called a few more times over the next half hour, but still no answer. It was around noon by now, and we thought that perhaps the office staff went to lunch. Over the next two hours, I continued calling, with no response. Wait, did we forget there was a snow storm? With local and regional trains cancelled, and roads not cleaned, how likely was it that the staff showed-up to work.

As my stress level started to increase, my partner had the practical idea to see if there was another number for the Administrator. There's a plaque with contact details at the entrance of the building, so we went to take a look. Thankfully, there was another number, and it even looked like a cell number! Maybe our luck was turning around. We called the Administrator, who answered promptly, and explained that there was no hot water or heating in the building. He asked if I had called the heating technician. Hummmm, I replied that I do not have the technician's number, and that I had been trying to call his office to ask for assistance, but that no one was responding.

> **B&B Owner Tip:** Collect all your emergency numbers for your building, and make sure you have the direct cell numbers to the experts so that no time is wasted when there is a problem!

Let me pause to introduce you to my partner, José, who has been part of the start-up of the B&B since I moved to Bologna two years ago. Born in Spain, he moved to the French part of Switzerland where he lived for 31 years. We managed a long distance relationship since meeting in 2012, until he decided to try Bologna, and moved when the B&B opened this past September.

I spent the next few hours waiting and wondering what was happening. José kept reminding me that there was no point worrying. As each hour passed with no news, I would call the Administrator, who would just tell me that they are working on the problem.

The guests for two of our rooms eventually arrived. They were two Spanish couples from Madrid, friendly and excited to spend their weekend in bologna. José took care of the check-in in Spanish, and had to advise them of the hot water problem. He completed the check-ins, and then joined me in testing the water every 15 minutes, hoping to feel the flow of hot water.

At around 9:00pm, relief finally flooded in, as I felt some warm water flow from the faucet - just in time for the arrival of our last guests!

They were a lovely couple from Berlin who had organized their trip last-minute, and had actually stayed with us at the beginning of the week. During their stay, they had mentioned that they would need to return to Bologna for their flight, and asked if we had a room available. After checking the calendar, I had confirmed that a room was free and blocked it for them.

I showed the guests to their room, and described some of the day's drama. I mentioned that if the snow continues, they may want to plan ahead when leaving to catch their flight the next day. They responded that it was no problem because their flight was in two days. Great! No -

wait a minute. Their flight is in two days? 'Yes, of course,' they responded. I replied that I thought they were staying one night. 'No, no. We told you that we needed the room for two nights. We're sure that won't be a problem right, you had told us that the reservation was fine...'

I admit that I froze at that point, just smiling, and mumbling that I would need to check. This was one of my nightmares...a double booking. Their room was only available for one night. There was already a confirmed booking via one of the main travel booking sites for the following night.

Did I really confirm two nights, or was something lost in translation? I found myself in a situation that I had meticulously tried to avoid since we opened. I always checked and double checked the availability of rooms whenever there was a private booking request.

By now, you may have understood that I'm a bit of a perfectionist. I take pride in the Bed and Breakfast, and in trying to create an experience that leaves our guests satisfied. I should have been able to prevent this from happening. I spent the next hour in front of my computer, wondering how I would tell the guests that the room wasn't available. What are our obligations to the guests in this situation? Was there a creative solution out of this mess?

> **B&B Owner Tip:** Never, never, never rely on giving a verbal confirmation for a private room booking. Always follow-up with a written confirmation that the guest can review and confirm, and to which you can refer if there are questions.

Seeing my mood worsening, José repeated that there was no reason to stress. 'Tell the guests that we do not have a room,' he suggested, 'and next time speak out right when the issue is raised.' I can't fault the advice, but it's also advice that is easier to offer when you are not the one managing the difficult situation.

I thought, maybe the weather would be the solution. Could it be possible that the guests arriving tomorrow would be blocked where they are? (Yes, I know - this was wishful thinking at its finest). I found their phone number, dialled it, and tactfully asked them if their arrival time may be affected by the storm. Their response brought some hope. they were not sure if their train will be operating, and they will call tomorrow morning to let me know.

The couple had left for diner, so I sat quietly waiting for them to return. When I heard the door unlock, I stood up, greeted them, and then described the situation. They were gracious and did not make a scene. However, they questioned why they should be the ones who would need to depart, instead of trying to finding a hotel for the new arrivals. We agreed to wait until after we heard from the new arrivals in the morning.

It was a very long and exhausting day, and I went straight to bed.

The next morning, I woke-up around 7:00am with the telephone ringing. The new guests were calling to confirm their arrival at 12:00pm. Perfect, the day is starting well, I thought. Now I just need to find a replacement hotel for our guests from Berlin. I started my morning routine wondering if we should consider compensating our guests for their troubles.

I placed the croissants and buns in the oven to start baking, and began to set the table. Suddenly, the power went out. Looking outside, we could see the snow weighing down the power lines. The lights were out in the post office across the street, and the alarm sirens from a store nearby start to scream in the early morning silence. It looked like the power was out in the whole block. My first thought was that I hoped the croissants and buns wouldn't be ruined. That was until we heard someone yelling out in Spanish. It was one of our guests.

José went to investigate, and then called out to me. Rushing to their room, we saw a large pool of water spreading across the floor, and spilling into the corridor and the room beside. Oh no, the Sanitrit!!! One of our rooms is equipped with a water pumping system called the Sanitrit. This solution is popular in Italy. Before the Sanitrit, it wasn't possible to create additional bathrooms in other parts of an apartment, if you could not connect the bathroom drainage pipes to the building's existing drainage tubes. With the Sanitrit, the pipes of the shower, sink and toilet of the bathroom are connected to a small box behind the toilet, which churns the water and waste, and pumps it through a small pipe that can pretty much follow any path through the apartment.

Ingenious right? Well, it needs electricity to run. We never had a situation where there was a blackout at the same time a guest was using the bathroom. That morning, the guests were taking a shower and using the toilet when the power went out. Without the motor of the Sanitrit working, the water had nowhere to go and overflowed, causing a large flood.

Grabbing towels, a mop, and even blankets, we started working frantically to collect the water. The wife was standing in only a towel, still wet, and her husband and friends were trying to help out with the flood. Minutes were passing, and we felt like no matter how much water we collected, the flood wasn't drying up. José went quickly to examine the bathroom and then called-out for a screwdriver. I rushed to bring him one, and he worked to open the cover to the box to the water valves. He had realized that the toilet wouldn't stop flushing and was letting out a constant flow of water. The only way to stop the flow was to shut-off the water, which he did. Now we understood why our mopping wasn't working. Why didn't the toilet stop flushing?

The clean-up continued, and the couple went to use the bathroom in the room of their friends to finish their showers. Suddenly, our doorbell rang. Wondering who might be ringing early on a weekend morning, I opened the door, and found a man asking if there was a water problem in our apartment. He's a neighbour from the apartment below, and he described that water was leaking from his ceiling and damaging his walls.

Did you ever wish that a day or even weekend never happened? Maybe it would have been better to never have gotten out of bed that morning. Sounding as apologetic as possible, I explained that we did have a problem, which we finally stopped, and that we would visit his apartment to see the damage once we finished the clean-up. This weekend was going to cost us...

B&B Owner Tip: Are you thinking of installing a Sanitrit or other system that relies on power? Make sure you have a backup power source that will kick-in when the power goes out, or a stop-system that will automatically shut the flow of water when the power goes out.

Learn also how to access the box where the water flows and churns the waste behind the Sanitrit. The Sanitrit system blocks when people throw items other than toilet paper into the toilet. No matter how much you ask guests not to throw any other products down the toilet, they still do. From tampons to condoms, you can bet that they will find their way to the motor. If you do not want to be waiting and paying for an idraulico (plumber) each time it happens, you might want to learn how to do it yourself.

After about 15 minutes, and a good deal of sweat from the clean-up, we felt a wave of relief as the lights turned back on, and the hum of the appliances restarted, including the motor of the Sanitrit.

While José continued with the flood clean-up, I started serving breakfast to our famished guests. After they were fed and left to prepare for their day, the couple from Berlin arrived for breakfast. I entertained them with a description of the morning madness, which they didn't hear from their room, thanks to the double insulated walls and doors. They were surprised about the Sanitrit however, as they commented that in Germany, the building code would not permit a system that depends on electricity to run, because of course there would be problems if a black-out occurs. Maybe Italians are not as disposed to foresight and prevention as the Germans. Certainly neither our architect, nor the construction firm responsible for the renovations (or even us), had anticipated our troubles that morning. The couple found the events of the last couple of days fascinating, and asked if we ever thought about writing them down and sharing them with others. Interesting idea...

Getting back to business, I advised them that the new guests already called that morning to confirm their arrival, and that we would help them find a new hotel. They seemed reluctant to make the move, and suggested a different idea – what if we contacted the online booking company to advise them that one of our rooms had flooded and ask their help in finding a new hotel for the arriving guests. This idea did seem like a good way out of this mess, so I quickly dialled the customer service number, explaining the issue. The booking representative responded that they would try to find an alternate hotel, and that they would contact the guests directly to make the arrangements. They advised that they would call me back to confirm.

Finally, some good news. I spent the next hour cleaning-up after the breakfast, and waiting for the phone call. It was getting close to 12:00pm, when suddenly, instead of the telephone ringing, the doorbell rang. Really? The new guests had arrived? I guess that there wasn't ever going to be an easy way out of this mess. I greeted them, and began to explain that we had a flood and that their room wasn't available. I was very embarrassed at this point, and am still embarrassed as I write this now. It was a white-lie. Should I have just been honest, and explain that we had an overbooking error?

I asked them if they were contacted by the booking company. They checked and saw that they received an email stating that we **overbooked** our rooms, and that a possible room was found in another Bed and Breakfast. Overbooked? Was this karma?

Regardless, I wanted to ensure that the new guests found a room that they would be satisfied with. I looked at the details of the recommended B&B, and was shocked when I saw that the price was more expensive, and that the B&B only had rooms with a shared bathroom. We offer three double rooms, each with its own private bathroom. I had assumed that the booking service would have found a comparable alternative. Having conducted a quick search on the booking site earlier that morning, I knew that there were better alternatives at the same rate. I advised them to decline the recommended room, and then found a room with private bathroom in a

4-star hotel in the city centre. Perfect! We made the new reservation, and I offered to take them to the hotel.

They were really gracious, and I continued to be very embarrassed for the situation. They did seem excited about the new hotel when we arrived, so I wished them a wonderful visit, and made my way back home feeling relieved.

I entered the apartment exhausted, and grateful that most of the drama was over. We would still need to deal with the water damage in the apartment below, and also figure out what went wrong with the overflowing toilet. We could take care of that later. José was also relieved that I seemed more relaxed. Although, he did take a moment to explain that the last two days were very tense, mostly in part because I had stressed-out from all the problems. He mentioned that he didn't leave his job and life in Switzerland to try living a year in Bologna, and be stuck in stress-filled situations. Did I mention that he had organized a sabbatical from his work, to test Bologna and the B&B? I responded that we all deal with problems differently, including him. Hopefully this type of weekend would be very rare.

Running the B&B is a new experience for both of us, and we still need to learn to manage the different types of problems that can occur, and also how to work with each other.

This is definitely going to be an interesting time...

2 Searching for the Right Home for a B&B

2.1
Wandering through the streets of Milano

I've set up home in Milano. Why Milano? I've been lucky to receive a job offer with a consulting company here.

Per our plan, I've moved to Italy first, to start my new job. I've been offered a job contract at 'tempo indeterminato' (a permanent contract), but it comes with a probation period. If it goes well, my husband will also make the move with our cats, in three months.

I've been able to find a rental apartment close to the metro stop De Angeli, only a couple of weeks after arriving in Milano. It's a small, one bedroom apartment in a quiet building, surrounded by greenery. While it isn't in the old city centre, it was available immediately, and I am only planning to stay for a few months. Once my husband arrives, we can explore Milano's neighbourhoods, and search for a more suitable apartment. The owners are also flexible and feel that they can trust us. They are the parents of my Italian teacher in Toronto, who is Milanese and had moved to Toronto a few years back.

When the weekends arrive, I put my walking shoes on and head out. Why take the metro to Milano's spectacular gothic Duomo, when I can explore the streets and appreciate Milano's urban architecture, which crosses periods like baroque, renaissance, liberty and more? By foot, I can still arrive to the Duomo in about 40 minutes.

My typical walk starts from the De Angeli metro entrance, and follows Via Marghera and then Corso Vercelli. I really enjoy watching the weekend routine of the Milanesi, as they enter and leave the many bars and shops lining the street. Once I reach Milano's outer ring, called the Cerchia dei Bastioni by the Milanesi, I follow Corso Magenta. The buildings along this street are much older, and it's here that I always pause to look at the renaissance church and UNESCO Heritage site, Santa Maria delle Grazie. This church is also home to Leonardo da Vinci's sublime Cenacolo, or Last Supper.

Traveler Tip: The Last Supper was painted directly on a wall in the convent adjacent to Santa Maria delle Grazie, and is actually about 4.6 meters tall and 8.8 meters wide. Some tourists mistakenly think that da Vinci's Last Supper is housed in Milano's Duomo, or they think that they can arrive at Santa Maria delle Grazie and see da Vinci's masterpiece without having reserved tickets. Only a small group of people is allowed to enter at a time, and tickets are in high demand. It's definitely worth a visit, but you will need to reserve tickets in advance with a group tour, or directly online at:

- http://www.vivaticket.it/?op=cenacoloVinciano[2]

Eventually, Corso Magenta reaches Milano's inner ring, known as the Cerchia dei Navigli. From this inner circle, I roam the streets of the old centre, until I reach the Duomo. Sometimes, I follow the ring along Via Giosuè Carducci, pass the Cadorna train station, and head towards Milano's renaissance Castello, to visit its ramparts and surrounding park. In the end, I always reach the Duomo.

It's during these walks, while contemplating the various sculptures decorating the facades of Milano's palazzi, that I finally feel like I am in the right place.

I've always had a strong desire to live in Italy. Now that I am here, it feels right.

Before the move, my friends and family would ask 'Why move to Italy? Living in Italy isn't the same as visiting it for vacation.'

After I moved, my Italian friends and relatives ask a similar question: 'Why would I move to Italy, when life in Canada is so much better?'

Better than what?

I try to explain that cities and countries have personalities that are just as diverse as the personalities of different people. What matters is to truly understand what's important for you to feel happy and fulfilled where you live. Living in a place with characteristics that better match your personality and interests can be life-changing. Passing years in a place that doesn't feel right can lead to misery.

If you have the urge to move, why not try it? There will be countless logical reasons telling you to stay where you are, and unless you are very wealthy, a major move isn't easy. I've always felt though that it is better to try it, than to live my life with the regret of an unfulfilled dream.

In Canada, I always had the sense that I was out of place.

First there's the weather. I love the sun and warmth – blame it on my southern Italian blood. The long frigid Canadian winters were too much. Each winter, I would promise myself that I would move and it would be my last Canadian winter. It's amazing how much a change of climate can completely affect your lifestyle. A warmer climate gets me out of the house. I am much more active and feel more energetic.

I also felt that I wasn't dedicating enough time for social activities and personal interests. It was too easy to fall into a workaholic routine...work long days, return home tired, and after an early dinner, veg-out on the couch until bedtime. Socializing was usually postponed to the weekends, and if you want to organize with friends, you would need to plan weeks in advance. I craved a routine where I could dedicate time, each day, to appreciate what was around me.

In Toronto, it seemed that people were less motivated and supported in finding a better work-life balance. With long working hours, and only 2 to 3 weeks of vacation a year, how does someone break out of the routine?

There is more to life than work.

There's a work conversation that has always stuck in my head. I was on an out-of-town project for a number of months, travelling each week from Monday to Thursday. I would spend long days blocked in a small conference room at the client's office with my colleagues and senior managers, and then pass the evenings in a hotel. One evening at around 7:30om, while still at the client's office, one of my colleagues asked, 'How about dinner at a restaurant tonight?' One senior manager looked up from her laptop and said, 'You aren't here on vacation.' This statement is wrong on SO many levels. Are we expected to work all night, until we go to sleep? Are we not entitled to me-time? What's wrong with visiting a local restaurant to have dinner, instead of eating room service at the hotel (at our own expense of course)? Why did she think she could control what we did with our time after work? This is just one of many examples, where I've watched people lose their balance. Part of the problem is that there are very few social norms or signals to help them understand that something is wrong. If you speak up, you are the one with the performance problem.

Another motivation to move is that the 'old' continent has always fascinated me. Compared to Canada, which has a relatively short history and a population that is just over half of Italy's population, the history and closeness of European countries captivates me. In just a couple of hours, I can be in a different country and experience a different culture, with its own food, language and customs. It's also easy to find yourself immersed in history going back hundreds or even thousands of years. I could spend a lifetime just exploring Italy, its historic towns and monuments, and its diverse coastal, inland, mountain, and island scenery. 'Day trips' or 'weekend getaways' have completely different meanings in Europe.

I also simply love spending hours aimlessly strolling around the town I call home. It doesn't matter how many times I may have walked down the same street, there is always something new to see, which I've never noticed before.

As I explore Milano, soaking up the summer sun, I'm excited to see where the next few years will lead. Once my husband arrives, we will start exploring the possibility of opening a Bed and Breakfast. The idea is simple – create a small venture that would give us the freedom and just enough income to be able to manage our own lives. It would be a lot of work, and maybe we won't succeed. It's worth a try though!

2.2
The journey or the destination?

The search for a place to run a Bed and Breakfast isn't going as I had hoped. I lost count of the times that I've told myself that finding the right apartment is impossible. We've hit continuous obstacles, and during the two years that we have passed in Milano, our relationship has also been crumbling apart. Maybe it would be easier to just close the chapter on the B&B dream.

Don't misunderstand me. I'm not saying that Milano wouldn't be a great place to start a Bed and Breakfast. It's a vibrant city that attracts large numbers of Italian and international tourists. It's also a fantastic city call home!

Maybe though, it isn't meant to be for us. I don't like to say that, as I'm not comfortable blaming 'fate'. We can influence our lives and create our own paths. For some reason though, we haven't been able to catch a break.

While I have been travelling out of town every week for work, my husband has spent his time taking Italian lessons, searching for the apartment for the B&B, and exploring other interests. Weekends are very busy, with our time split between apartment visits, chores, and social activities.

However, each time we've visited an apartment that has potential, we would do our research and discover that it isn't suitable.

We did think that we finally found the 'perfect' apartment, near the end of our second year here in Milano. We even made an offer, and it was actually accepted!

If you are thinking of opening a Bed and Breakfast in Italy, before making an offer on an apartment or house, take the time to understand the real estate market, and to get informed of all the requirements for running a B&B.

There are different regulations to meet, if you want to open a Bed and Breakfast that is legally compliant. For example, there are the general construction by-laws for a residential apartment. A B&B in Italy is considered an activity run in someone's home, and you will need to comply with all the residential by-laws. These by-laws are very specific in detailing numerous requirements for the living space.

You will of course visit many apartments that don't comply with these by-laws. These apartments were likely developed before the latest by-laws were written, or they were renovated without permits. If you want to buy a 'non-compliant' apartment and don't have plans to renovate, then there are no immediate problems. However, as soon as you want to legally renovate, all the non-compliant details must be changed. These by-laws dictate minimum requirements like your main kitchen must have a window, the principal bathroom must have a window, each bedroom must have a window, you cannot place an entrance to a bathroom that is directly accessed from the kitchen, and much more.

You may have started to note that the number of windows in the apartment is very important. Our plan is to create a B&B with three bedrooms for the guests, plus our own bedroom. That's already four windows. Another two windows would also be needed, one for the kitchen and one for a principal bathroom. We have visited many large apartments where it wouldn't be possible to create all the rooms, simply because there aren't enough windows. Obtaining permission to cut out another window in a building, especially a historic building, is almost impossible.

Don't try to do it all on your own either. Make friends with an Ingegnere or Architetto (engineer or architect). Both of these professions are involved in design and construction. In Italy, the line between the role of an Ingegnere and Architetto is very blurry. While both professions focus on creating a home that is well constructed, an Architect supposedly also considers how a space meets the lifestyle of the owner. It's usually up to you to choose between an Ingegnere and Architetto, but it may also depend on the type of building. Either professional should be able to describe the laws that need to be met.

You will eventually need an Ingegnere or Architetto to draw up your renovation plans, so finding one who can help you from the start will save you time afterwards.

Some friends had introduced us to an Ingegnere that works in our neighbourhood. He is very knowledgeable and always honest in giving his opinion. Once we developed a good understanding of the by-laws, we started to visit apartments on our own. If an apartment has real potential, we will then return with our Ingegnere for a second visit, to ask whether he thinks the space can realistically be converted into a B&B.

You will also need to pay attention to structural limitations. For example, are there any important structural walls that can't be moved, which might limit how you can use the space? We have also been adamant that each bedroom of the B&B should have its own bathroom. The vision is to design a comfortable space where guests will have the privacy and comfort of a hotel, while also feeling like they are at home. We are not interested in offering discount accommodations, and a private bathroom is an essential feature. Unfortunately, it is very rare to find an apartment with more than one, or even possibly two bathrooms. The plan for our space would need four bedrooms and four bathrooms. Consequently, it's important to understand if there are any restrictions with moving walls, and installing additional plumbing connections.

Windows, walls and plumbing.... After many visits, we've become discouraged with seeing great apartments that don't meet these basic requirements.

Construction by-laws aren't our only concern. After all, we are intending to open a Bed and Breakfast, and there are also tourism industry laws to respect. The laws governing B&Bs in Italy are actually defined by each region, and not by the state. There is no common national law. In Milano, we needed to understand the laws for the region of Lombardia.

In these laws, there are requirements like minimum sizes for bedrooms, and bathrooms.

So, the focus is on windows, walls, plumbing, and the square meters of the space.

After understanding all these requirements, we thought that we just need to concentrate on finding an apartment with the right layout...right? Wrong!

The Bed and Breakfast law for Lombardia describes that you can run a B&B in your home. In fact, you are required to live there, to consider it a B&B. However, even though you are legally allowed to run a B&B in your home, it doesn't mean that the other inhabitants in your apartment building want you to. Your legal right is overruled by the condo rules.

Our Ingegnere advised us from the start to always ask for a copy of the condo rules, to check if there are any restrictions to how an apartment can be used in the building. These condo rules are usually written when the building was first constructed, and could have been changed over time. Changing a rule is always complex, usually requiring a majority vote by all the owners.

As we visit apartments, we explain our B&B plans to the sellers' real estate agents, and ask to see the condo rules. It's not a simple request though. Most of them never have a copy readily available, and need to ask for a copy from the condo administrator. Many agents have tried to convince us that it isn't necessary. They've told us that the regional laws permit a Bed and Breakfast, so there isn't an issue. Some agents have also said that we don't need to worry, because there are other owners running B&Bs in the same building.

Once we get a copy of the rules however, almost every building we've visited in Milano has a rule stating that operating a 'pensione' in the building is forbidden. *Pensione* is an old-fashioned way of describing a short-term stay accommodation, and you still can find the word used in beach-side towns where people offer holiday rental apartments. The agents, wanting to make the sale, have explained to us that a 'pensione' isn't the same as a B&B. But they aren't the legal experts.

Our Ingegnere continued to caution us to avoid a building with this rule, as any unhappy resident of the building can potentially take us to court, to have us stop the B&B. Even if the judge rules in our favour, it would likely be a lengthy and expensive court process.

Fed-up with hearing these conflicting opinions, I decided to write an email directly to the Region's tourism office responsible for the B&B law, asking for clarification. A week later I received a reply from one of their legal representatives (wow, in just a week!), which agreed with the opinion of our Ingegnere. They said that it would be up to the judge to decide if the word 'pensione' applied to a B&B, as it could be interpreted as a general word for all accommodations. There is a risk that a judge can rule against us.

Would you risk investing all your savings on an activity that could be stopped by a spiteful neighbour?

At least now, when a real estate agent would tries to tell us that a condo rule against a 'pensione' isn't important, I can respond that it is, based on the legal advice of the region.

We've wondered why most apartments have this restriction in their rules. The only explanation that our Ingegnere has suggested is that there was a period in Milano when there was a boom of temporary room rentals for brothels. Fed-up, residents in the buildings may have tried to stop these activities by forbidding them in the condo rules. Who knows if this is true.

After almost two years searching in Milano, we finally struck gold after seeing an apartment in Piazzale Loreto. It was an ideal location because it was right on the metro line that leads straight to Milano's Duomo. We liked the surrounding neighbourhood, as it offered good shopping, bars and restaurants. Piazzale Loreto also has important historical significance. It was the place that Italians had taken the body of Musolini at the end of World War II, and hung it upside-down for everyone to see.

The apartment was located right on the circle of the Piazzale, and was in a small building of 8 floors. The beauty of the apartment was that it took up the space of the entire floor, and the elevator entered right into the apartment. In fact, each floor only had one apartment. It was also the perfect layout with the right number of bedrooms and bathrooms. An initial sketch by our Ingegnere showed that only minor renovations would be needed, to move a couple of walls and refresh the bathrooms.

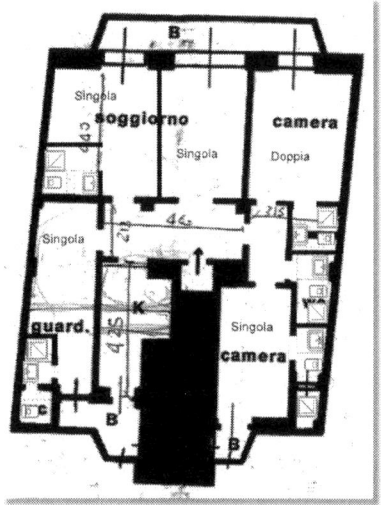

We asked to see the condo rules, and did find the familiar phrase forbidding a pensione. However, the owners seemed convinced that with the small number of owners in the building, most of whom they knew personally, we could successfully get a special approval to run the B&B. The owners were a brother and sister, who had inherited the apartment from their mother, and they seemed willing to negotiate.

When we presented our offer, we included a condition that the sale would proceed only if the condo board approved the B&B. The owners weren't worried, and offered to help facilitate the approval process for us.

The owners did ask for a condition on their side. Their condition stated that if they had to cancel the sale, they would not be required to pay the customary penalty. Normally, when you make an offer, you provide a cheque for a sum of money, say around 5 or 10 thousand Euros, to show you are serious about the purchase. If you cancel your offer, you lose this money. However, if the owners cancel the offer, they must pay you back double the amount.

Were the owners just being cautious? We didn't think much about it, and we agree to their condition. We also added an additional condition that if we cancelled the offer for any reason, we wouldn't be penalized either, and they would return our deposit.

Over the next month, we worked with the owners and the condo administrator, to organize a meeting with all the other apartment owners, where we would present our plan for the B&B and request their approval. Everyone seemed positive that the meeting would be successful. We were getting very excited. It was finally going to happen. Maybe this would also be a positive catalyst to help get us beyond our relationship issues.

A few days before the condo meeting, we received a call from the real estate agent. She advised us that the owners were withdrawing from the sale. WTF?

Apparently, the brother and sister had a stepfather, who was claiming that he also had partial ownership rights to the apartment, and he was not in agreement with the sale.

How could another 'owner' suddenly appear? Why didn't the real estate agent know about this before?

The brother and sister advised the agent that they could not sell, and that they were planning to take the stepfather to court to claim damages for his obstruction. Now that they had a real purchase offer, they intended to go to the judge claiming that the stepfather not only didn't have the right to partial ownership, but that his actions have lost them a potential sale, valued at our offer amount of course. In other words, this wasn't a new issue with their stepfather. It was an ongoing drama, and our 'offer' gave them that legal edge to claim for damages.

We felt naive, stupid and used.

We finally understood why they asked to include their 'condition' to not be penalized if they cancelled. They were expecting it.

It was a massive waste of time and energy, and it was demoralizing.

Months have passed since that debacle, and we continue to search, with no luck. The issues in our relationship are also hitting a peak. I honestly don't know where our future is heading.

2.3
One second of fame in Italy

We've made the news in Italy, even if they didn't spell my husband's name right.

My husband and I have been together since 1998, and we married in Canada in 2009. Italy, however, doesn't recognize our relationship or marriage.

The day after I arrived in Milano, I went to the city's Anagrafe office (civil registry) to request my 'Carta d'identità', the Italian identity card. You may be imagining a plastic card similar to a driver's licence, which other countries in Europe issue to their citizens. In Italy however, the card is retro. It's an oversized paper card folded into two, with your cut-out photo laminated against the paper. It's bulky, and ruins easily carrying it around. It also becomes out-of-date practically as soon as it's issued, because they include your address at the time of issue, but they don't re-issue a new card when you move.

After waiting my turn, I approached the booth, and mentioned to the city employee that I just arrived to Italy and required the Carta d'identità. They went through the list of questions to collect my personal details. When they came to the question on whether I was single or married, I replied that I am married to a man, and that our wedding was in Canada. The employee looked-up at me and said 'Italy does not recognize gay marriage, so here you are single', and typed the word 'libero' (free or single) on my card.

That was expected. We knew that in Italy, we would be giving up the equal rights that we were accustomed to in Canada.

We had done our research on immigration options, before arriving. It was simple for me. I'm a dual Canadian / Italian citizen. My mother became a Canadian citizen shortly after she arrived in Canada, when she was a child. At that time however, dual citizenship wasn't permitted, and she had to relinquish her Italian citizenship. My father, on the other hand, grew up in Italy and moved to Canada in his 20s. Since coming to Canada, he has never applied for Canadian citizenship, and has always remained a landed Italian immigrant. As a child of an Italian citizen, I had the opportunity to have my Italian citizenship recognized. I took advantage of this opportunity when I was 18, when I requested my first Italian Passport from the Italian Consulate in Toronto. Maybe the idea of moving to Italy has been lurking around for a long time ;-).

For Djordje, the most practical solution was to arrange a student visa. The visa lasts up to a year, and he would need to be enrolled and attending a school. We arranged for him to take Italian language classes. The course hasn't been cheap, but it's a great opportunity for him to become fluent. The downside is that each year, he needs to sign-up for a new course and reapply for the visa.

One alternative could have been to find a job and apply for a work visa. However, unless you have a very specialized skill, companies usually avoid offering jobs to candidates who don't already have a long-term visa, as they don't want to become involved in the visa application process. We thought that maybe once we open the B&B, we could arrange for him to be 'employed' by the B&B, and he could apply for the work visa.

If only Italy recognized our marriage, then we could have saved all this trouble and simply apply for a spousal visa.

Recently, we heard about a gay couple who married in Spain, one Italian and one not, who received a visa for the non-Italian spouse in the region of Emilia-Romagna. It was the first time that this happened in Italy. We didn't know how they succeeded though.

Unfortunately, the visa application process is neither crystal clear, nor consistent across Italy. Visa applications are made at the office of the 'Questura', in the city where you live. The Questura is the local headquarters of the state police. While the visa eligibility guidelines are defined by the state, there seems to be a certain amount of discretion left to each office on interpreting them.

The home of the Italian LGBTI association, Arcigay[3], is in Bologna, which is the capital of Emilia Romagna. I thought that if anyone would know how the couple succeeded in getting the visa, it would be Arcigay. They may even offer legal counselling assistance.

I called the association, and explained that we are looking for legal advice for a same-sex spousal visa. They replied that they cannot help, but they can refer us to a small group of lawyers, who have been working independently to follow different legal avenues to support LGBT rights. The group is called 'Associazione Radicale Certi Diritti[4]' or radical association for certain rights. That's an interesting name. Why is the idea of equal rights still considered 'radical'?

I contacted the group, and was introduced to one of their lawyers. Over a series of conversations, and even a visit to her home in Lago Como, she explained the strategy. It was simple. The Italian laws did not recognize same-sex marriage, and it would be a waste of time trying to get our marriage recognized. Instead, as a member of the European Union, Italy has certain obligations related to the free circulation of European citizens and their families. Italy's refusal to provide a visa to gay spouses means that the country is not meeting its obligations to free circulation.

So, we would make the application citing Italy's European obligations. With the lawyer's help, we completed all the forms.

A couple of days ago, Djordje and I went to Milano's Questura to submit the request. We waited our turn, and when our number was called, we approached the counter. We explained that we are a married couple applying for the visa, and that per the legal advice of our lawyer, we are submitting the application based on the European law of free circulation. The representative took our papers, told us to wait, and went to speak with his superior. About 5 minutes later, he returned with his superior, who said 'Your visa request is approved on the basis of freedom of circulation in Europe. However, Italy still does not recognize your marriage.'

Absolutely perfect! We were there to get a visa for Djordje, and not to have our marriage recognized.

Since then, our story has been printed in a number of newspapers across Italy[5].

Our friends have been congratulating us on this fantastic success, and we even had a couple of calls from journalists asking for interviews.

But the truth is that it's heartbreaking. We are separating.

Since moving to Italy, our relationship has fallen apart. Maybe the move to Italy was a catalyst, or maybe it simply uncovered the cracks hiding beneath the surface. Our relationship wasn't perfect, but I naively believed that our marriage would be for life.

The deceit has been crushing me. Who is this person exploring other 'interests' when I'm out of town? Most weekends have become either scenes of frustration and anger, or we evade confrontation to keep an uncertain truce.

Maybe he thinks I'll turn a blind-eye. Or maybe he's instigating me to make the decision to end the relationship. I don't know.

All I know is that for the last two years my physical health has deteriorated, and my mental health is in worse shape.

I stopped believing in our relationship a few months ago. During a work trip to Switzerland I met José. We passed a couple of days together, which seemed genuine and positive. I realized I had forgotten what it felt like to be happy.

I can continue analyzing and justifying what has happened for endless pages. I have so much sadness and anger boiling in me, and maybe writing it down would be a better outlet than suppressing it all. That would be a different book though.

The bare truth is that I've made the toughest decision I have ever believed possible - the relationship needs to end.

I'm also leaving Milano. I've recently found a new job, and my new employer is located in Emilia Romagna. So I've decided to move to the region.

I'll miss exploring Milano's vibrant neighbourhoods, and spending hours socializing with friends over aperitivo.

I will also miss my husband.

Our time here has been adventurous and full of energy, but it has also been the most difficult two years of my life.

I hope that this is the right decision. At the very least, it will be a new start.

2.4
Bologna – a city of water?

You may have started to realize that I'm a bit of a control freak. I like to have an objective, lay-out a plan, and manage the way until the goal is reached. However, my time in Italy keeps reminding me that control is an illusion. At some points in the journey, it's better to stop paddling, and let the waves take you to where you need to be.

Did I ever think I would call Bologna home? Never. I knew nothing about Bologna before moving to Italy. It's not a destination that most people think of when planning a trip to Italy.

I've ended up here through a series of coincidences. The new company I work for is located in a smaller town, about 30 minutes north of Bologna. I spent a few months renting an apartment in that town, but it wasn't for me. The town is beautiful, but way too small and quiet. After living in Milano, I've learned that I really enjoy being able to step out of my home and find myself in the centre of a vibrant city, surrounded by places to see and things to do.

So I decided to give Bologna a try. It means a commute to the office, but the train system is convenient, and I can walk to the train station.

Now that I am here, I recommend to everyone planning to visit Italy, to stop by Bologna.

If you haven't heard much about Bologna, the first thing that may come to mind is Spaghetti Bolognese. See my story about Spaghetti Bolognese, to avoid that mistake ;-).

Those who know something about Bologna may associate it with tortellini, mortadella, medieval towers, the oldest university in Europe, and its portici (endless arcades, that cover most of the sidewalks in Bologna).

But did you know that Bologna is also a city of hidden water?

Bologna has an intricate canal system, which was developed between the 13th and 17th centuries. They connect with the rivers Reno and Savena, and eventually the river Po. Their original purpose was to bring water into the city to run the mills, and to provide water for the different industries, like textile factories and tanneries.

There are 5 canals still left, but most are hidden, as their waters flow beneath the streets and buildings of the city. The canals were covered rather recently - in the 1950s, when the city implemented a new urban plan to rebuild Bologna after the damage from World War II.

There is one canal though, which provides you with a window to how life in Bologna looked like for hundreds of years. It's called Canale Delle Moline.

Canale Delle Moline enters Bologna's old city centre at the intersection of Viale Giovanni Vicini and Via Monaldo Calari. You can view its waters at this entrance, right beside the church Santa Maria e San Valentino della Grada. The canal flows past the grada di ferro, or iron barrier, which is still connected to part of the old city wall behind the church, and was used to block enemies from entering the city.

Across from the church, there is a simple building with a couple of windows. If you look through, you will see one of the locks that controls the entrance of the water into the city.

The canal then flows under Via Della Grada and continues under Via Riva di Reno. If you are walking along the route of the canal, and are in the mood for some good gelato, stop by Gelato Capra[6] in Via Riva di Reno, to taste one of their great flavours, made from latte di capra (goat's milk). My favourite flavour is 'Carruba', or Carob. If goat's milk isn't your thing, you can also take a quick detour to the Cremeria della Grada[7] in Via San Rocco for the more traditional creamy Italian gelato.

Continuing down Via Riva di Reno, you will reach the intersection with Via delle Lame. Here, there's a church sitting in the middle of Via Riva di Reno, called Santa Maria Della Visitazione al ponte delle Lame. This church was originally built on the bridge over the canal. During the plague of 1527, the Bolognesi would pray to an image of the Madonna on a tabernacle on the bridge. After the plague ended, the church was constructed to house the image of the Madonna. Behind the church, when the canal was still open, the women of Bologna would go to the canal to wash their family laundry. You can find some old black and white fotos showing this daily routine (and yes, 'fotos'...there is no 'ph' in Italian and I am starting to appreciate some of the Italian spelling).

Bologna, Lavandaie in via Riva di Reno. Genus Bononiae.[8]

Follow Via Riva di Reno for a few minutes, until you reach where it ends and meets Via Galliera. At this intersection you will find the church Santa Maria della Pioggia (pioggia is the Italian word for rain). It was originally known as San Bartolomeo di Reno, but its name was changed in honour of an icon of the Virgin Mary, considered miraculous. The Bolognesi believed that the Virgin helped during a severe drought in the 16th century, and afterwards they would come to this church to pray for rain during dry periods.

Across the street from the church is a fantastic shop called the Drogheria della Pioggia. It's one of Bologna's historic shops, and there you can find almost anything you might need, from home products, to sweets, to balsamic vinegar.

> **Traveller Tip:** If you're in Bologna, and can't squeeze in a short visit to Modena, the home of Aceto Balsamico (balsamic vinegar), stop by one of Bologna's specialty food shops to buy some Balsamico from Modena. Real Balsamico from Modena is nothing like the store bought variety, which is usually artificially aged through a cooking process. Balsamic truly aged in barrels can offer a variety of exquisite flavours, just like great wine. You can find a great selection of Balsamico at various price ranges at the Drogheria della Pioggia.

To reach the next and most popular viewing point of the Canale Delle Moline, follow the small street of Via dei Falegnami, cross Via dell'Indipendenza, and continue along Via Augusto Righi. The first street to your right, on Via Augusto Righi, is Via Piela. Turn onto Via Piela, and after a few meters, you will reach a small window on the wall to your right. Look through the window, and you will see the following surprising view.

This view has a special meaning for me. If you look closely at the foto, you will see that I've drawn a circle around one of the balconies. This is the balcony of the apartment I've been renting since I moved to Bologna. It's a simple one bedroom apartment, but I love it. The tall angled wood beam ceilings give it a spacious feeling, and the view from the balcony is spectacular.

When I arrive home and enter my apartment, it feels like I'm in a different place and time in Bologna. My front windows open into the tranquil internal court of the building, and my two back balconies on the canal. The flow of the water insulates against the hustle of the city life, and even though I am steps from Via dell'Indipendenza, the apartment is a peaceful refuge.

This is my view from the balcony looking towards the window. José says that the facades of the buildings need to be restored. I disagree. They're absolutely perfect!

I haven't had to adapt or become accustomed to living in Bologna. The transition has felt effortless.

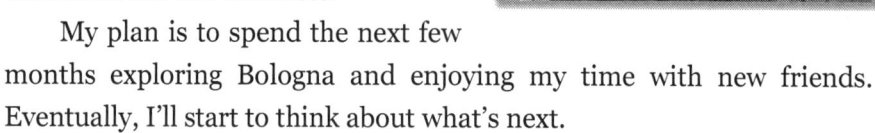

My plan is to spend the next few months exploring Bologna and enjoying my time with new friends. Eventually, I'll start to think about what's next.

Tonight though, it's time to go and meet new friends for aperitivo.

2.5
Cosa facciamo stasera?

'Cosa facciamo stasera?' 'What are we doing this evening?' This question is becoming a daily ritual. After working all day, there are a few options: eat at home and veg-out on the couch, go for a walk around the old centre, or meet friends for aperitivo and maybe even dinner.

After a couple of months living in Bologna, the last option is becoming a 7 day-a-week routine. This isn't a complaint though. It's one of the aspects of Italian life I was hoping to find, and Bologna has this trait moulded into its DNA.

I've found that Bologna offers something extra, compared to some of the more renowned Italian cities like Florence, Venice, Rome and Milan. I'm not criticising these other cities. Rome is Rome - it's a unique clash of ancient and modern life, in a stunning and chaotic city. I return continuously for short 3-to-4 day visits, but living there would be too stressful. I also absolutely love wandering the small alleys of Venice, and contemplating the art and richness of Florence. They are like walking through open-air museums. Their beauty and history are inspiring, and they open a window into how Italian life was in the past.

However, when it comes to finding the right city to call home, I think I prefer a city that offers both a beautiful historical ambiance, and also invites you to participate in the daily social life. I would like to savour home cooking in restaurants full of locals, or sip a drink on a bar terrace while eavesdropping on the local gossip. This experience isn't readily available in many cities. I've visited a number of beautiful city centres across Europe that become deserted in the evenings, because no one actually lives in the centre anymore. Just look up at the apartments as you walk by, and you will see that most are dark and uninhabited. Either the locals have moved out to more inexpensive communities, or they rent their apartments as accommodation to tourists. A city centre should be lived in, especially its historic core.

Bologna, on the other hand, invites you into the real daily Italian life and culture. Italians live, work and play in the centre. While the centre is actually quite large, you can reach any part conveniently by foot, and you will always find people walking its streets. I love that I can exit my building and be in the middle of a city bustling with energy.

The Bolognesi also seem to be naturally social. Life here is about appreciating the simple moments with friends over an aperitivo of prosecco, a tagliere of salumi (a wooden board with a selection of cured meats), or a hearty plate of pasta.

When I say 'Bolognesi' though, I do not mean Italians born and raised in Bologna who have a family history in the city that goes back generations. So far, I've only met a couple of 'true' Bolognesi, and have started to joke, saying that true Bolognesi are a rare breed. Bologna instead has become the adopted home of many Italians from all over Italy, who either came as a student and decided to stay, or have made the move for work.

I haven't figured out yet what drives the social atmosphere that you feel as you walk through its streets. Is it the youthful university crowd? Maybe, but you won't find university students spending their money on a glass of wine or prosecco. Is it because many Italians from other regions have adopted Bologna as their home, and are open to making new social connections? Possibly, but Milano is also a city of immigrated Italians, yet the same welcoming feeling is hard to find.

To give some perspective, my ex and I passed an entire year in Milano before we finally developed a circle of friends. Every weekend we would visit the same bars, but never had a local start a conversation with us. They all seemed to socialize within small, closed circles of friends. Even the bartenders were reserved, only asking for our order, and never saying 'Hi, it's good to see you again.' After a year, we were at one of the usual bars, and an Italian from Rome visiting his friends started to chat with us. From there, he introduced us to his 'circle', and we finally broke through into the social scene. Once inside, the 'circle' is very social and we were very busy with aperitivi, dinners and more.

During my second weekend in Bologna, I went to a bar that organizes a Sunday evening aperitivo. I was there with my ex, who was visiting for a few days. While standing outside the bar with our drinks, a guy, well groomed and in his 40s, started a conversation. He offered his name, Domenico. Domenico grew up in Pavia, and his mother is originally from Calabria, like my parents. His partner's from Puglia. We spent the evening having a great conversation. They were interested to hear what brought me to Bologna. Domenico mentioned that he was organizing a birthday party at his apartment for a friend in a couple of days, and invited us to the party.

Wow – that was very generous. I was grateful for the invitation, and excited to meet other Bolognesi. After Milano, I didn't expect to make friends this quickly. I accepted the offer, bought a nice bottle of wine as a gift, and arrived to the party nervous and hoping to make a good impression.

Domenico lives just outside the historic centre, near Porta San Felice, an easy walk of about 20 minutes from my apartment. His apartment was tastefully decorated – with a mix of antique and modern decor, and a living room wall completely covered in a patchwork of original artwork. The apartment was also full of guests, mingling and chatting over glasses of prosecco.

I learned that Domenico is an architect, and the friend he was hosting the birthday party for had a clothing boutique in Via San Felice.

It was a fantastic evening, and I met many people. I'm horrible with names, and couldn't remember most names. However, I did exchange cell numbers/WhatsApp and Facebook with a couple of people. Italians love social apps, and Facebook and WhatsApp are the basic survival necessities if you want a social life.

A few days later, I received an invitation to aperitivo at a bar in Via del Pratello, from one of the people I had met at Domenico's. I remember having already walked down Via del Pratello during the day, but it didn't make much of an impression as it seemed like a quiet residential street. Strolling down the street that evening, I realized that it's one of Bologna's epicentres of social life. The street was lined with bars and restaurants that were full of people socializing.

I could really get to love this street. Although, I wouldn't want an apartment there. The hum of hundreds of people socializing until well past midnight would drive me crazy.

There, over aperitivo, I made some more new friends, a few who actually live in apartments in Via Del Pratello. One in particular, Domenica, felt like a kindred spirit. Like me, she is a child of Italian immigrants, who grew up in another country, and decided to move to Italy. Her parents had moved to Germany, where Domenica was born and raised. Domenica however moved to Italy after high school, to study fashion in Rome. She lived there a number of years, and then moved to Bologna for work, where she has been living for over 20 years. She also recently separated from her ex, and was looking to rebuild her social life.

Since encountering Domenico and Domenica, I've been meeting them regularly for aperitivo or dinner, passing the evenings chatting, and learning about life in Bologna. They have large social circles, and are eager to help me make new friends. I am also learning that there is no shortage of bars and streets that offer a great social ambiance. Some of the places that are becoming my favourites include:

Via del Pratello: This street is known as Bologna's liberal bohemian street. In the evenings, it is very lively, with a diverse, casual crowd. There are a number of great bars and restaurants to choose from, some of which even organize live music. The residents also host a fantastic street party every April 25 for the Festa Della Liberazione, the commemoration of the end of World War II.

Via Belvedere: This is a small street, hidden just behind the Mercato delle Erbe[9], Bologna's covered fruit and vegetable market. There are a number of bars, some historic and some new, where you can meet friends and enjoy a great selection of wines, cocktails and more. The street is even more vibrant in the summer time, when all the bars arrange tables and chairs on the street, and the crowd continues all evening long.

Via Pescherie Vecchie: This is a small alley beside Piazza Maggiore, and is full of spots to grab a glass of wine and something to eat. It is also home to Bologna's outdoor market, with shops that sell traditional products from the region like parmigiano, prosciutto, mortadella, and more. Try some of the traditional tigelle. They are small round flat bread that you cut into two, and fill with cured meat, or cheese, or both. There is also a small fish market called Pescheria Del Pavaglione[10], which sells fish during the day, and offers a fantastic aperitivo in the evening, where you can order wine and eat various small dishes prepared with either cooked or raw fish.

There is a smaller side street off of Via Pescheria Vecchie called Vicolo Ranocchi. There you can find one of the only remaining true osteria, called Osteria del Sole[11], which dates back to 1465. An osteria was originally a place that only served drinks, not food. If you wanted something to eat, you needed to bring it with you. This spot continues this tradition, and there is always a crowd of people inside and outside, chatting with glasses of wine in hand.

Now that I've passed a couple of months in Bologna, I am very comfortable saying that it's a city where I can be happy and call home. The only challenge I face now is how to avoid burning out between a full-time job and the nightly ritual of aperitivo...haha!

2.6
A needle in a haystack?

The family living in the apartment keeps following us around. We are a group of over 20 interested buyers, who have arrived to the scheduled appointment to view the apartment. As we move from room to room, the family members trail closely behind.

The apartment is located in a building on Via S. Isaia, a beautiful street in the centre that features Bologna's typical low-rise architecture and portici, which blend together in warm hues of yellow. One disadvantage is that the street is a primary traffic route, in and out of the centre. Maybe some good sound-proofed windows would be enough to block out the street noise.

It's in great condition, with elegant wooden floors and trims. It's also very large, about 170 square metres (1,800 square feet), and has an impressive terrace of 60 square metres (645 square feet). A terrace in the city would be a fantastic luxury!

One of the interested buyers started a conversation with a family member - the wife. I overheard the wife explain that they could no longer afford the payments for the apartment and are forced to leave. It's sad, the sale isn't by choice. In fact, the apartment has been repossessed, and the Tribunale di Bologna (the city's courthouse) is facilitating an auction.

It feels awkward walking around the apartment, while knowing that they are being pushed out of their home. I wonder what they're thinking as they watch all these strangers inspecting their rooms and belongings. The apartment is still fully decorated and furnished with a lifetime of possessions. I'm not sure that I would have chosen to be present for the viewing if I was in their position.

The main draw for the large crowd of potential buyers is the price, of course. The base bidding starts at 220,000 Euros, which I estimate is much less than half of what an apartment of this size would be listed for in Bologna.

Inspecting its rooms, I admit that it would be a great place to call home. But I'm not really feeling the fit.

Am I looking to buy an apartment as a home or a B&B? I'm not 100% certain yet. I don't know if it is still financially possible, but I haven't been able to give-up the idea of opening a B&B. So I've re-launched the search, this time in Bologna.

Will I spend the rest of my life in Bologna? I'm learning not to plan that far in advance. I'm focusing on the short term. For now, the city feels right. After about six months, it's already home. I could easily pass the next five to ten years here, and I am comfortable with the idea of investing my savings in a property in Bologna.

I also don't know whether José will be involved. We are really good together, but we are at very different points in our lives, not to mention we live in different countries. There have already been a couple of times when I thought that our relationship would end due to the distance.

José left Spain and moved to Switzerland when he was young, and has spent over 30 years building a life there. He has a stable job, a great circle of friends, and an apartment in a small, peaceful town. If he continues working in his job, he can retire comfortably in about 12 years, with a reasonable pension.

About a year has passed since we met. At the beginning, I actually considered moving to Switzerland. His roots are planted much firmer than mine, and it would be infinitely simpler for me to make the move. So, during the first 6 months, I passed many weeks in Switzerland. My work responsibilities at the time also made the frequent trips possible.

Slowly though, I began to understand that moving to Switzerland wasn't right for me. I would sit on the couch looking at the quite hillside outside José's windows, and feel depressed. The lifestyle and routine in Switzerland is almost a mirror of that in Canada. It took me almost a decade of effort to make the move to Italy happen, and I realized that I cannot give-up what I've found, and return to the old routine. I believed that I would need to end the relationship. There would be no way that

José would abandon his life in Switzerland to move to Italy, and I was not happy in a long-distance relationship.

We had some emotional and dramatic conversations – the drama mostly from my side. I joke that it's because of my spicy Calabrese blood. The reality though, is that I am re-learning how to manage my emotional conflicts. I haven't yet found my balance, and still miss the maturity and poise that I used to rely on before the troubles began with my husband.

José however seems willing to keep all options open. His philosophy is to take it step by step. He explained that he is open to considering a move, if it is well thought through.

I'm not convinced though that he will be able to make the drastic change. The Italian and Swiss lifestyles are polar opposites. While he's originally from Spain, the Swiss life seems more attuned to his personality. Regardless, he has encouraged me to re-launch the apartment search.

To start, I need to understand if a B&B is still a realistic objective. I need to learn about Bologna's real estate market, and what's possible in my budget. I also need to research the regional laws for running a B&B.

There are the usual channels to search for an apartment, like visiting the different real estate offices around the city, and combing through listings on the major Italian websites.

Some friends also mentioned the 'aste immobiliare', or property auctions. Properties that have been repossessed are put up for auction in Italy. The auction process is managed by each city's courthouse, like the Tribunale di Bologna[12], and new listings are usually published online.

> **B&B Owner Tip:** The auctions can offer a potential source of low cost properties - if there isn't a bidding war. Be careful to understand all the conditions related to the sale process, which will be outlined in the documents that accompany the property profile. For example, viewings can be restricted to only a single group visit, and the bidding process is strictly defined, including payment obligations.

I've decided to keep my options open, and have included property auctions in my search. However, finding the right apartment for a B&B is already a challenge using the traditional channels. Hoping to find the right apartment with all the requisites, which has been repossessed and is being sold cheap in an auction, seems like a fantasy. I don't really believe in luck.

This apartment won't work though. The 'L' shape layout, with the large entrance foyer and hallways, wastes a lot of the square meters needed for the bedrooms and bathrooms.

It's time to leave and let the other interested buyers continue their inspection.

2.7
The Notaio

I remember watching the movie '*Under the Tuscan Sun*[13]' before moving to Italy, and laughing at one of the comical scenes where the main character, Frances, is in the office of what seems like the Notaio, who explains that the legal description of the land is 'two oxen, two days', and hands Frances the keys of the house, even before the money is transferred. After all, it's not like she can steal a house. It makes me laugh every time, but my experience is completely different.

When my ex and I purchased our home in Toronto, we paid a lawyer to prepare the paperwork and register the purchase. Lawyers however, are not involved in a house purchase in Italy. Instead, the responsibility to conclude the purchase lies with the 'Notaio', or notary.

The profession of the Notaio is somewhat coveted in Italy, as not everyone can become a Notaio. There are a limited number of Notaio positions set for each city or province, which are managed nationally by the Ministry of Justice. When positions become available, the Ministry launches a competitive process that involves multiple exams. Successful candidates would then need to relocate to the city or province where that vacant position resides.

This means that you need to select a Notaio that has authority to operate in the town where you have purchased your home. Depending on the size of the town, your options may be limited. It's not an open and competitive market, so you will also find that there are a number of services that seem to have predefined price-tags.

B&B Owner Tip: When the time arrives to find a Notaio, contact at least two or three different Notai to ask for a 'preventivo', or a quote. You can find the list of authorized Notai for your town on the site www.notaio.org[14]. The preventivo will include very important information such as the amount of the taxes you will need to pay on the purchase, as well as the fees for activities like registration. While most parts of the preventivo will have set fees, there is still a little wiggle-room to select the Notaio who offers the cheaper rate for her or his time. You may be able to save a few hundred Euros.

For an accurate quote, you will need to provide clear details on your citizenship, Italian residency status, if it's your first or second home in Italy, who is the seller, and what type of property you are buying. All these factors can have a significant impact on the percentage of taxes you will need to pay on the sale, which could range from 2% to 10% of the sale price.

Once the owners accepted my purchase offer, I contacted three Notai to ask for a preventivo. In the end, I selected the Notaio who was originally suggested by the seller's real estate agent. He had previously helped me by answering questions about the amount of taxes I would need to pay. His preventivo also came in cheaper than the other two.

Oops, did I forget to mention that I've made an offer to buy an apartment?

After an owner accepts your offer, the most frustrating activity will become managing the timeline up until the 'rogito', which is the final date when the contracts are signed, money is exchanged, and you get the keys. While you would have indicated in your offer a date for when the sale will be closed, it might not actually be the final closing date. The final closing date is dependent on a number of factors, and you will need to do your best to coordinate them all.

These include:

- Approval of your mortgage: If you need a mortgage, Italian banks do not provide pre-approvals. The approval process comes after the owner has accepted the offer. As part of this process, the bank will send a representative to confirm the value of the property, which in Italy is called the 'perizia'. Then, the mortgage request will be assessed by the head office. No matter how much I tried to persuade them, banks in Italy will not commit to a date by which they will provide their decision. The bank may say that it should be completed within 30 days, but it can also take longer.
- Contract Preparations & Property Checks: It's the Notaio's responsibility to ensure that the property has been registered accurately with the city, that the ownership is clear, and to conduct other checks. They will also prepare the purchase contract, or 'l'Atto di Compravendita'. The Notaio will usually start their work after you have confirmed that you have been approved for a mortgage. After-all, why should they start work sooner, if you might be refused the mortgage?
- Everyone's Availability: You will have the fantastic pleasure of trying to get everyone to agree on a specific date and time for the rogito, where they will all need to be present at the Notaio's office to sign the contract. This includes juggling the availability of the Notaio, and the current owner. If the property was inherited, then there may be multiple owners. In my case, there are two brothers who inherited the property after the death of their third brother. Also, if they are married, the spouses will likely want to be present. Lastly, if you are getting a mortgage,

then the Notaio will need to prepare a formal mortgage contract between you and the bank. This contract will be signed at the Notaio's office on the day of the rogito by you and the bank's Director, so you will also need to coordinate with the Director's schedule.

Since you will have already committed to a closure date in your original offer, you will likely ask yourself, 'Should I wait until the mortgage is approved before I coordinate the date of the rogito?' In theory, the rogito should be concluded before the offer's closure date expires, yet the whole timeline is dependent on the mortgage approval. I worried that if the mortgage took excessively long to approve, then there would not be enough time to organize the rogito, before the closing date in the offer expires. It was like a 'chicken and an egg' question.

My advice is to set the date for the rogito as soon as you can. The reason is simple. You will encounter many situations in Italy, where work will only get done if the person is under pressure. For example, with all the files piling up on the desk of the bank employee responsible for reviewing your mortgage request, why would you expect that your file gets processed in chronological order. Who knows what priority your file has been given, especially when other files might come in under tighter deadlines. Light a fire under their behind by setting the date of the rogito. This way, the employee will work to meet a specific date. It will also give you leverage when you keep calling the bank to ask why you haven't yet heard back about the mortgage approval.

If you've been successful in herding all your cats, then you will only need to wait patiently for your date to arrive. In the meantime, it's always a good idea to check-in regularly with all the parties, in case there are any questions sitting on their desks, waiting to be answered.

On the day of my rogito, I walked into the Notaio's office feeling like I stepped backed into the early 1900s. It was a simple space, surrounded by wooden shelves filled with old dossiers and books. The Notaio's workspace was an antique looking wooden desk, and positioned in front of the desk were enough old wooden chairs for all of the participants. There wasn't a computer in sight. The only computer I noted was that of the assistant seated out by the main entrance. As I was the first to arrive, I couldn't help but snap a quick foto before anyone else entered. The foto at the beginning of this chapter is the actual one I took.

While the rogito in the film '*Under the Tuscan Sun*' was an exceedingly quick affair, mine was a bang-my-head-on-the-desk lengthy and dull event. It's the responsibility of the Notaio to explain the content of the contract. However, this doesn't mean clarifying the key points. It means reading every single written word in the contracts. That was 13 pages of Italian legal text, which incorporated sections from the historical purchase contracts of the apartment. Oh, and because I was also getting a mortgage, the current owners left the room, and the bank Director and I had to sit through the Notaio reading another 19 pages of legal text for the mortgage contract. I'm not a coffee drinker, and I was desperate for a shot of energy to keep me focused and patient throughout the whole event.

With all the contracts read and everyone's signature on the appropriate dotted lines, I am now the happy owner of a 150 square meter (1615 square feet) apartment in Bologna, in desperate need of massive renovations.

2.8
What did I get myself into?

This is the foto I've taken after entering my apartment for the first time as the new owner, fresh from completing the ceremony of signatures at the Notaio's office.

I'm sitting on the floor of what is to become the future kitchen and living room. It's a quiet, celebratory moment, but inside I'm bursting with contrasting emotions, as I sip some champagne.

The euphoria is sweet. I did it! I actually purchased an apartment that I would turn into a Bed and Breakfast. While it took less than a year to find and purchase the apartment since moving to Bologna, this day is at least a decade in the making. It has taken years of hard work, night-classes, career changes, language lessons, and accumulated savings. My family isn't wealthy, and this is a moment of self-made pride. I admit to a few outbursts of laughter as I sit on floor. I just can't believe it.

Thankfully, the euphoria is dominant enough to suppress the panic bubbling in the background. I just signed a 30 year mortgage contract. Between the money I invested for the down-payment, and the money I will need for the renovations, I will be using all of my savings. And I mean all of it. I even cashed in my pension savings, taking a very painful tax hit of 25% on their total value.

The renovation budget estimated by my architect better be right. If the money runs out, I'm not sure what options I'll have. I am still working full-time. However, my salary will be dedicated to the new mortgage, and to my ongoing living expenses, which include the monthly rent and expenses for the apartment I am currently living in.

I also have this nagging sensation that if something can go wrong, it will. Is this all too good to be true? There are too many unknown variables. How will I manage the renovations and business start-up in a country that is known for its drama? How will I balance everything while also working my full-time job? What happens if the renovations get blocked by something unforeseen and expensive? What if the other inhabitants of the condo become upset and make it their mission to make my life difficult?

Take a deep breath.

The previous owners have removed what little furniture had been sitting in the apartment, and this large room feels empty now. The apartment is also very silent. The only sound is coming from me as I shift my position while sitting on paper towel that I've placed on the floor to protect my clothes from years of accumulated dust.

This is also a bittersweet moment.

José, is still in Switzerland. We see each other only on the weekends, and this day was a weekday. He has been part of the apartment search, and in fact, is the one who first found the apartment on one of Italy's real-estate websites. He wasn't able to be here to celebrate with me, and this just reminds me that I am not happy with the long distance relationship. Can the Bed and Breakfast really be the solution to establishing a home together? Will he really make the move to Italy after 30 years in Switzerland, where he had his friends, a stable job and benefits, and less than a decade left to a comfortable retirement?

And how did I get to this moment without my husband. We were together 14 years, and I always believed that we would grow old together in Europe. We worked so hard to get to Italy. I still don't understand what went wrong.

My champagne glass is almost empty. Do I want a second glass? Not really. There is no time to waste in endless thought and psychoanalysis. I got this far, and there is a Bed and Breakfast to create!

2.9
My guilty pleasure

January is my month of depression. It's not because it's the coldest month in Bologna. Compared to a Canadian winter, an average of -2ºC to 5ºC feels more like springtime. It's also not because the days are shorter and darker, where the sun struggles to peak over the building tops, and the city is regularly covered by waves of nebbia, or fog. I actually love walking around Bologna when it's blanketed by fog at night, and the street lights illuminate the medieval arcades with their secretive yellow glow.

The real cause of my depression is that the Cremeria Funivia[15], my favourite stop for gelato in Italy, closes for the entire month. Yes, I realize this sounds childish. It's just that throughout the year, I can get my weekly fix of their rich and creamy gelato. Ok, let's be honest, I usually indulge more than once a week. In January however, the owners and employees take a well-deserved break.

This chapter may be one of my more trivial ones. However, I have a demanding sweet tooth, and the Funivia is the best. I can't wait to suggest to all the guests of the B&B to try their gelato.

Each time a friend mentions a different favourite spot in the city for gelato, I make a point of visiting it, to do a taste comparison. However, I always return to the Funivia. For my taste-buds, nothing else compares. José describes it as the caviar of gelato.

Bologna has developed an understated selection of amazing artisan gelaterie and cremerie. I say 'understated' because while Bologna is known as Italy's food capital, its reputation is based on its pastas and cured meats. Most Italians will likely point to Sicily as the home of the best gelato. While I've tasted granite in Sicily that are sublime (a type of fruit-based slushy), I haven't yet found gelato comparable to the Funivia. Although, maybe it's because I'm always too distracted eating all the fantastic Sicilian cannoli.

If you ask people living in Bologna where the best place for gelato is, half of them will likely recommend La Sorbetteria Castiglione[16], and the other half Cremeria Funivia. I'm on team Funivia. The term cremeria is fitting, because at the Funivia, the milk-based gelato is much creamier and richer, and also not icy the gelato you find at a typical gelateria. This means that the temperature of the gelato is not as cold, and your tongue doesn't become frozen, so the flavour is more intense. My favourite flavours are their pistacchio, alice (marscapone), and cioccolata al rhum (rum). Put it all together on a crunchy wafer cone, with some liquid chocolate poured into the base of the cone, and I'm in heaven!

Don't get me wrong, it's worth a taste tour of the smaller artisan gelaterie around town. I enjoy the deep cioccolata fondente (dark chocolate) at La Cremeria Della Grada, as well as the specialty flavours made from goat's milk at the Gelato Capra, like Carruba (carob). It's also a delight to taste the homage to the regional cuisine at Pellegrino 1936[17], with flavours like crema with aceto balsamico (cream with balsamic vinegar) and pieces of prosciutto di parma, or parmaggiano reggiano with cooked pears, cinnamon and walnuts.

In the end though, I always seek out the Funivia. My philosophy is that if I'm going to consume the calories, I prefer to eat the best gelato!

The countdown anxiously continues until the Funivia reopens in February...

2.10
Let the demolition begin!

No wait, first we need to celebrate! I am ecstatic and emotional to have reached this point.
- Apartment suitable for a Bed and Breakfast found – CHECK!
- Architetto (architect) hired and blueprints completed - CHECK!
- Renovation company selected and work ready to start shortly - CHECK!

This is happening...and I've decided to host a little party of about 40 acquaintances in the apartment, before the demolition begins.

It's going to be a simple party, with makeshift tables using construction materials, a buffet of finger food and drinks served with plastic dishes and cups, and spray paint. Yes, spray paint, for people to go a little crazy and paint the walls that will be demolished with some urban art, or 'tagging' as they call it in Italy.

No, a demolition party is not a tradition in Italy. It's just something I cooked-up with Domenico, my Architetto, to share this milestone with friends, and to start creating some awareness of the B&B. Yes, it's the same Domenico that I meet just after a couple of weeks in Bologna, who had invited me to the birthday party he was hosting in his home.

I've taped a large printout of the blueprint of the future B&B on a wall. This way, people can visualize what is going to change. I am also going to ask everyone to sign it, as a memento.

The renovation will be a massive amount of work. The only parts that will remain original include the wall separating the living room from the rest of the apartment, and the marble floor in the living room. Everything else will be demolished, and rebuilt from scratch.

'This could actually work', I thought. In fact, that was the same thought I had the first time I visited the apartment.

José first spotted the apartment on one of the popular real estate listing websites used in Italy. (A couple major sites are www.casa.it[18] and www.immobiliare.it[19])

> **B&B Owner Tip:** In Italy, it isn't customary to hire a real estate agent to help you search for the right home. I think the simple reason is that the buyer is already stuck paying a substantial amount in fees. For example, as a buyer, you will need to pay a portion of the seller's real estate agent fees. Your portion usually ranges between 2.5-3.5% of the selling price (plus 22% IVA sales tax on the agent's fees). You will also pay the Notaio's fees for preparing the contracts, registering the sale, etc. Don't forget about the purchase / transfer taxes. All these fees are not included in the selling price, and you will need to add them on top of the price. The seller does get the better end of the deal.
>
> This is a point that continues to irritate me. You do all the work to search for your home, and once you find a place you like, you need to negotiate with a real estate agent who represents the interests of the seller more than your interests. Then, if you finally get through the ordeal, you need to pay their fees.
>
> You can of course hire the services of another real estate agent to help you search for your home. However, this is just an extra cost on top of everyone else's fees that you are stuck paying.

I remember taking a look at the web-link of the apartment listing that José sent. The small drawing of the plan showed a layout with some of the basic requirements for a B&B. There were already two bathrooms, one of which seemed long enough to be able to split into a third. There were also three bedrooms, with potential space for a fourth, and there were enough windows for all the bedrooms and at least

2 bathrooms. Did I also mention that the apartment had two entrances, one which could become the entrance for the B&B, and the other the entrance for our personal space? Perfect! That was another key requirement of mine. I wanted to be able to maintain a minimum amount of personal privacy, and avoid having clients entering and leaving from my space.

The price was also very promising.

Up to that point, I was becoming more and more negative about the B&B dream. I kept thinking that creating a B&B was no longer a possibility with my budget. When my ex and I arrived in Italy, we thought we had enough funds to create the B&B. However, after separating, we both ended up with only half of our savings.

The housing market in Italy had slowed over the last few years, due to the prolonged economic crisis. Prices were lower, but they didn't seem low enough for my budget. I visited a number of apartments in Bologna with great potential, but in the end I had to let them go as they were priced too high. I was also shocked at the number of derelict apartments I visited, where the owners were asking top dollar for apartments that weren't even liveable without considerable renovations.

I called the real estate agent listed on the advertisement and arranged to visit the apartment.

I arrived on-time for the appointment. From the outside, the building looked unremarkable. It was a newer building, and didn't have a notable façade, nor did it resemble the typical architecture of other more historic buildings in Bologna. However, as I entered the apartment and started to explore, I thought 'oh my god - finally an apartment that could work...and the price might be within budget.'

I tried not to show any excitement to the agent. I explained to him my plan to create a B&B, and that before I could understand if the apartment is suitable, I would need a couple of things. First, I asked the agent to email me the condo rules, to make sure there weren't any restrictions against operating a B&B. Second, I wanted to arrange a follow-up visit with my Architetto, to get his opinion on the viability of the layout I was envisioning. For example, would it be possible to create the 4th bedroom and bathroom, and were there any important structural walls or pillars that couldn't be moved?

The condo rules came through a couple of days later... and there were NO restrictions. Wow! After all the challenges in Milano, this seemed too easy. I arranged the second visit with Domenico, my Architetto, and then a third with José. There was consensus that the apartment had potential to be converted into a B&B. I was more than ready to make an offer!

Presenting the offer was somewhat painless. I showed up to an evening appointment at the agent's office, ready with my offer price. The agent advised that the owners would negotiate only within a limited range, as they had already reduced the price a couple of times over the last year.

I responded that the amount of renovation work needed to make the space liveable, even just for me, was significant. The apartment hadn't been lived-in for about a decade. The current owners were two brothers who inherited the apartment from a third brother, who had passed away. The original owner was a lawyer, who used part of the space as his legal office, and the other part as his home. After he died, their mother lived there for a short time, until she also passed. Since then, the apartment remained closed, until the two brothers finally decided to sell it.

They had their asking price for the apartment, plus they wanted an additional 50,000 Euros for a parking space inside the building. 50k for a parking space, when parking on the street is free for residents?

Compared to all the other apartments I visited, the price for the apartment was reasonable, and considered its condition and the needed renovations. If I cashed in all my registered retirement savings from Canada, I thought I could make it work.

I presented my offer for the apartment and the parking. We went back and forth in discussions. In the end, the agent thought that the owners would consider my offer for the apartment, but thought that the offer for the parking space was too low. He finally suggested that we prepare two separate offers, one for the apartment and one for the parking. This way, the owners had the option to decline the parking offer and accept the apartment offer.

Fine with me. I signed the offers, and a couple of days later received the call that the owners accepted the offer on the apartment and not for the parking.

Fantastic! I later learned that there was a communal gated parking area between the apartment building, and two other adjacent buildings. As a resident, I was eligible to park one vehicle there on a first-come basis, at no extra cost. Interesting how the agent and previous owners forgot to mention this benefit when they were asking for 50K for a parking space.

Regardless, the purchase was a success! Compared to all the obstacles in Milano, everything finally felt like it was falling into place. What I had thought wouldn't be possible was now becoming a reality.

The guests are starting to arrive, and there is some spray-painting to do in honour of the pending demolition!

Dreams to make come true

2.11
The break

Everything is moving fast, really fast.

It's March, and the renovations will start in a couple of weeks. The target is to complete all the work, and be ready to open the B&B by the beginning of September.

My friends think I'm pazzo (crazy) with the opening date, considering that the entire apartment needs to be demolished and rebuilt. They also remind me that there is August, a month where pretty much the whole country shuts down for vacation. We'll see.

I've never been busier, and once the renovations begin, it will only get more intense. I'm not sure how I'll juggle my full time job, monitor the renovations, and prepare the start-up of the B&B. The list of things to do during these next few months keeps me awake at night.

There are also some important decisions that need to be taken.

With just six months to opening, I need to understand how the operations of the B&B will be managed. Running a B&B with three rooms and three bathrooms will be a lot of work. There are the reservations to manage, daily breakfast to serve, check-ins and check-outs to conduct, and of course the rooms to clean.

José has indicated that he will consider moving to Bologna. It would be a massive change. Sometimes I'm grateful that he would think of uprooting his life to be here with me. Other times, I feel guilty. What happens if it doesn't work out? Maybe he'll discover that Bologna, and Italy, isn't for him, just like I realized about Switzerland. What happens then? Would he be able to return to his job and life?

Considering a move is brave. Actually making the decision and taking the actions to plan and implement the move is an extreme challenge.

Time continues to pass quickly, and I haven't seen any progress.

Will José actually make the move and be here by September, in time for the opening? If he ends up choosing not to come, how will I run the B&B? I have the option to quit my job and manage it on my own. Or, maybe I can hire someone - but what are the obligations and costs?

These questions have become a regular discussion topic during José's weekend visits. Both feeling the pressure, the conversations recently turned into arguments. That is, up until a few weeks ago, when José decided to break it off.

Since then, we've been speaking. José has taken the time to reflect at his own pace, and he's reached his conclusion – he has decided to test living in Bologna. His plan is to request a sabbatical from work, which would start in September, and if it goes well, he will formally resign from his job.

Now that I know the direction we are taking, I can focus on getting to the destination. There's no time to waste!

3 The Renovations

3.1
Why should laws be logical?

I've signed the Atto di Compravendita, paid the taxes on the purchase, and am now the owner of an apartment in Bologna. When it comes to money management, my focus has turned to the renovation budget. Of course, there are the usual utility expenses and monthly condo fees, but they should be manageable. Some friends have also reminded me of the annual property taxes, but I thought that there was no need to worry. I would just pay the tax bill when it arrives in the mail, right? WRONG!

My first wrong assumption is that I should expect to receive the tax bill in the mail. Around the time of the first mandatory payment, I heard a couple of friends moaning that their tax bill never arrived. Apparently, it's somewhat normal that your bill never gets mailed out. Regardless, you are obligated to pay your property taxes by each of the two deadlines, one mid-year and one at year-end. How do you know how much to pay if you don't receive your bill? Before searching for your crystal ball, grab the phone and call your Commercialista.

The Commercialista is like an accountant, and is a life-saver in preparing your personal and business income taxes. The Commercialista can also help you understand your property tax obligations.

The property tax bill is made up of numerous parts, and the calculations are dependent on multiple factors, like the registered value of your home. Other factors include state and city laws, both of which are constantly changing. One of the biggest challenges in Italy is a lack of stability in tax laws, and it is the almost impossible job of the Commercialista to stay informed. Your Commercialista can help calculate your property taxes, and prepare the forms needed to make the payments via your bank. Listening to my friends, I realized I was clueless and needed to do something. So I called my Commercialista.

My second mistake is that I assumed that since my apartment is the first and only property I own in Italy, I will be automatically taxed on it as my first property. I didn't know about the dependency with my registered address.

In Italy, you need to declare your residency or 'residenza' with the city's registry or 'anagrafe' office. Your residenza is the address of where you regularly reside. You are legally required to declare your residenza whenever you change your address, and there are very important services that depend on your residenza, like selecting your family doctor.

The process of declaring your residenza can become one of those convoluted experiences that leaves you to shake your head in awe. While there are some small differences between cities, the common parts of the process include:

- Declaring your new address to the city, usually via an in-person visit at the anagrafe office.
- A verification by the city that you actual live at your new address.

You may be wondering, how can the city successfully verify where you live?

Usually, within 30 days from when you declare your new address, the city will send a 'vigile urbano', a member of the municipal police, to knock on your door and visually confirm that you live there. I say usually, because a visit isn't guaranteed. At this point, you may have some additional questions like:

- What happens if you aren't home? Well, in some cases, you may receive a call directly from the vigile to arrange another time. The vigile might also just try another day. Or, the vigile may decide to not pass by again.
- If the vigile doesn't actually visit, how do you know if your residenza was registered or rejected? Sometimes a city might send a letter of confirmation. Other times, they will tell you that

if you haven't heard any word after 30 days from when you made your declaration, you can consider it registered.

Regardless, you can always return to the anagrafa office after 30 days, to ask for a letter that confirms your residency. You will likely need to do this anyway, as a verification letter is needed for important activities like opening up a bank account and getting a mortgage.

It's a complex process, all designed to ensure that people truthfully declare their residenza. However, because your residenza has significant implications, people are very selective of where they are registered. I know a number of people who have their residenza declared in cities where they don't actually live.

I've always been curious as to why they would go through the trouble, and from this painful lesson, I finally understood. Your residenza is also critical for your property taxes.

My plan has been to continue living in the apartment I'm renting until the renovations are completed. I purchased the apartment in January, and the renovations started in April. The work should be done by September, and naturally, I planned to go to the city's anagrafe office to change my address once I moved. 'What's the rush', I thought.

When I called my Commercialista, she requested the documents needed to prepare the property tax calculations, including confirmation of my residenza. It's near the end of April, and the renovations are well underway. I explained that I haven't yet changed my residenza as I'm still living in the rental apartment. 'That's a problem', she replied. She then explained that since my residenza is registered at another address, I will be taxed at more than 3 times the rate, because the property I purchased is not considered my primary residence, but a second property.

'You must be joking', I replied. 'How can the apartment I purchased be my second property? I only own one property, and need to pay taxes solely on that property. I don't pay property taxes on the apartment I'm renting.'

'The definition is based on your registered address,' she explained, 'and not on the number of properties you own.'

My Commercialista then suggested that I go to the city's anagrafe office and declare my new address as soon as possible. This way, I will need to pay the higher tax rate only for these first few months.

I organized some free time, and went to visit the city's anagrafe office in my 'quartiere', or neighbourhood. There, I explained to the city employee that I purchased a new apartment, and would like to change my address. The employee asked if I will be present when the vigile passes to confirm the residency. I responded that renovations are being done to the apartment, and I may not always be there.

'Is there at least a working kitchen and bathroom in the apartment?' she asked.

'They aren't yet ready,' I replied.

'Unfortunately, without a working kitchen and bathroom, the vigile will not consider the apartment liveable, and will not accept the change of address,' she explained. 'You will need to wait until the renovations are completed to change your residenza.'

'Just perfect', I thought sarcastically. Now, I'll be stuck paying taxes at a crazy rate for at least six to eight months, if the renovations are completed on time.

If I had taken the time to become informed from the start, I would have gone straight to the city to change my residenza when I received the keys to the apartment, before the renovations started. That way, the vigile would have seen an apartment that was somewhat liveable, with an old kitchen and bathroom, and I would have saved more than one thousand Euros in unnecessary taxes!

Moral of the story – don't assume that the laws operate with the same logic as your home country. Ask questions, and then ask more, until you know what to do!

3.2
Il Computo Metrico – your renovation bible

Another variation to the original work plan just arrived via email. The renovation company is asking for an extra 1,700 Euros, to install the Sanitrit system in the bathroom of one of the bedrooms. They also need to run the sewage pipe up along the wall and across the ceiling, to the main discharge pipe located on the opposite side of the apartment.

I have no problems paying extra for new or unexpected work. This variation is really irritating however, because the work isn't unexpected.

Back when I first visited the apartment with Domenico, my Architetto, we discussed that the bathroom for this particular bedroom would be too far from the main sewage discharge pipe to make a normal connection. For a normal connection, the pipe from the bathroom would need to run along the floor, at a slope that is high enough to guarantee the flow of the sewage. Just looking at the distance between the potential bathroom and the building's sewage discharge pipe, we always said that it would be impossible, without substantially raising the level of the floor.

To get around this problem, Domenico suggested the Sanitrit system. This system takes the water from the shower, sink, toilet and bidet, breaks up any waste in the water, and pumps it out through a pipe. The diameter of the pipe is much thinner, and the pump system enables you to run the pipe up walls and across ceilings, until it connects to the main sewage pipe.

So if this was always planned, why wasn't it included in the original quote, and why do I need to pay extra now?

I called Domenico, and explained that I just received the variation request. 'Why do I need to pay extra for something that was always planned,' I asked.

'The Sanitrit system for the bathroom wasn't included in the Computo Metrico, and naturally it would be an extra cost,' he replied.

Il Computo Metrico – it's your bible that describes the entire scope and cost of a planned construction or renovation.

This isn't a critique of the Computo Metrico. The document is extremely effective in defining a renovation.

The Computo Metrico lists all the work that will be needed, from the start to the finish. It includes sizes and quantities, like the total square meter of tiling needed, or square meters of walls to be demolished and rebuilt. It also lists all the supplies and products that will be purchased and installed. Most importantly, it identifies the price for each row of work described, and for all supplies/products that will be needed.

The complete Computo Metrico is defined and agreed to before the start of the work. It even needs to be finalized before you submit your renovation plans to the city, because you will need to declare your Architetto **and** the renovation company you have selected when you send the blueprints to the city. Both the Architetto and the representative of the renovation company need to sign the submission, and prove they have the necessary registrations and insurance. By signing, they are also providing a quality guarantee of usually 1-2 years after the work is completed. If there is an issue with their work, they are expected to correct the problem.

We are in Italy, and yes, we know of examples of friends who hired workers to renovate, where there were no invoices, no submissions to the city, and of course cash payments. While they will pay less for the work, and will also avoid paying taxes, they are accepting greater risk. If there's a problem that surfaces after the work is completed, you can find yourself paying more for the re-work. It's very complicated renovating an apartment in an existing building. You don't have a crystal ball to see if the work today may cause a leak in the apartment below six months afterwards. Or if the air-conditioning doesn't run like it should the next summer. It's an enormous relief to be able to call the renovation company, and have them fix the problems.

B&B Owner Tip: Check with your Commercialista and Architetto for information on the latest renovation tax rebate programs. For example, as I am renovating my 'first home', I am eligible for a tax discount on the purchase of building supplies and fixtures. Instead of paying the typical purchase tax of 22%, I only pay 10%. All the purchases are usually made by the renovation company, so negotiate with them on what they can purchase for you.

The Italian government also currently offers a very good multi-year income tax rebate for home renovations, up to a predefined maximum. To take advantage of this rebate, it's very important to follow the process for paying the work invoices through your bank.

It's your Architetto's responsibility to draft the Computo Metrico, and it is only as good as his or her experience, and the level of detail included. Renovation companies will provide a quote against each line of work and supplies described, so the more detailed and precise the description, the more accurate the quote will be.

I love detail. Abstract work estimations only lead to arguments, so I'm a great fan of the Computo Metrico.

That being said, you can't foresee all the work. Expect to pay at least an extra 15% on top of your quote for unexpected work. After all, you can never really anticipate what you may find when you tear out floors or walls in an old building. You will also need to budget for costs that are not part of the work estimate of the renovation company, like installations and connections by utility companies.

You may have noted that I mentioned that the costs of all the supplies and fixtures are also included. This means that before the sign-off of the Computo Metrico, you should have selected all your items like flooring, bathroom fixtures, and even possibly light fixtures.

Architetti in Italy generally consider themselves holistic designers of a home, and may include interior design consultations as part of their services.

Domenico has become a good friend, since I first met him at the local bar when I moved to Bologna. He loves his work, and is very passionate and articulate about design. Maybe he was only helping a friend, but together, we visited many stores, where I selected all the supplies. He has great taste and made good suggestions, especially concerning modern decor, with which I have less experience. However, I also have a very clear vision for the B&B, and we had some great debates. For example, his idea of a clean, modern apartment was to have the same ceramic tiling running through the halls, bedrooms and bathrooms. To me, that sounds more like a school or hospital. I want to create a feeling where, when the guests open the doors to their bedrooms, they feel like they are stepping into their own private space. As I was paying, I had the final decision, and had fun selecting different tiling - haha!

To have full control of your budget, I recommend that you also select as early as possible, the other contractors you may need to undertake work that your renovation company doesn't do. Will you need a new kitchen? A renovation company is not responsible for installing a kitchen. You will need to purchase and have the kitchen installed by a company specializing in kitchens. I also contracted a carpenter to create a corner bar in the hallway where guests could prepare coffee or tea, and purchased the bedroom doors with extra soundproofing from an 'infissi' company, which specializes in door and window fixtures.

Once you and your Architetto agree to the Computo Metrico, it's ready to be sent to a few renovation companies for quotes. I sent it to three companies, two of which Domenico had already worked with.

I selected the mid-priced company as they were committed to completing the renovations by September. Domenico had also worked with them numerous times, and highly recommended them based on their quality, speed and professionalism.

I have nothing but praise for them. The work started in April and the plan is to be finished in September. This is a complete gutting and transformation in just over five months. The renovation manager, Raffaele, is very detailed, organized and attentive to quality. The company also has a complete team, including plumbers and electricians, and doesn't rely on subcontractors. This means that Raffaele is in full control of the availability of the workers, and the quality of the work.

The Architetto's work doesn't end with preparing the blueprints and the Computo Metrico. In Italy, they usually assume responsibility to manage the overall renovation. Domenico is overseeing the progress and quality of the work, and is also managing the timing of the installations with the other contractors. He visits the 'cantiere', or work-site, multiple times a week, and collaborates with me and the renovation company to resolve any issues or obstacles. He's been a lifesaver!

Getting back to the issue of the extra quote for the Sanitrit system, I asked Domenico 'Why wasn't the Sanitrit system included? We had always discussed that we needed to install it.'

I was almost certain that it was in the Computo Metrico, and scanned the text in my copy. I couldn't find it though. In the plumbing section, it only described the general work for creating four bathrooms.

'We couldn't have been sure that the Sanitrit system was the best solution until we tore out the floors', he responded. 'If the space under the floor was deep enough, we could have run a normal pipe to the main sewage discharge pipe'.

'Maybe - but that was VERY unlikely', I replied. 'Since we always discussed that we needed it, I assumed it was in the Computo Metrico. In fact, it would have made more sense to include it in Computo Metrico, and then have a nice surprise and savings if the space was deep enough. I am budgeting for unexpected costs, but this wasn't one of them. My total budget keeps growing, and I am worried I will reach my limit.'

'Look, the company quoted a price to complete a normal bathroom. Whether the Sanitrit system was included before or now, you would naturally need to pay the additional cost for the system, and to run the pipes.'

I just gritted my teeth and breathed.

Lesson learned - go through every word of the Computo Metrico before finalizing it, to make sure that EVERYTHING you expect is actually included. You know what they say about assumptions...

3.3
What - no spaghetti bolognese?

If you visit Bologna expecting to eat authentic spaghetti bolognese, turn right back around. There is nothing authentic about spaghetti bolognese. The spaghetti Bolognese you are familiar with was likely invented outside of Italy, even though you may even find it on the menu of some restaurants in Italy that cater to tourists.

Instead, in Bologna you will find that any trattoria of good quality will serve authentic Tagliatelle al Ragù.

First, forget about spaghetti. Spaghetti is not a type of pasta from Bologna, nor from the region Emilia Romagna. This region has perfected **tagliatelle**, which are flat egg-based noodles, slightly wider than the fettucini-type noodles that you may know. The tagliatelle should of course be hand-made.

Emilia Romagna has a rich history of home-made pasta, noted in many historical cookbooks, like Pellegrino Artusi's quintessential cookbook *La scienza in cucina e l'arte di mangiar bene*[20], from 1891. If you are able to read in Italian, you can actually download a free ebook copy of Artusi's celebrated cookbook on the following site: http://www.pellegrinoartusi.it/il-libro/[21].

After a year in Bologna, it's easy to become spoiled with the many different varieties of hand-made pastas, and we now tend to be disappointed and a bit snobbish if a restaurant serves store-bought packaged pasta. We always ask a restaurant if they offer pasta made in-house.

In Bologna, there are a number of small shops that prepare and sell a selection of hand-made pastas, which you can purchase and bring home to cook. One of our favourite shops is Pasta Fresca Naldi[22], located on the vibrant and bohemian street, Via del Pratello. It's a small shop run by a few ladies who make fresh pasta daily. They also offer a delicious selection the typical pasta dishes, which they serve ready-to-eat. You can order these dishes as take-out, for an impromptu picnic lunch, or you can take your dish to one of the bars nearby, where you can enjoy your meal of fabulous fresh pasta with a glass of wine.

Travelling around Emilia Romagna, you will likely note the diversity in the words used for pasta. For example, the small pasta shops in Bologna will use the word 'sfoglia' to refer to fresh pasta. In other regions in Italy, 'sfoglia' is a type of flaky desert pastry. In some restaurants, you will also see pasta's listed under the heading 'minestre'. 'Minestra' in the rest of Italy, usually means a type of hearty soup with different vegetables.

> **Traveller Tip:** If you want to get your hands dirty and learn how to make your own pasta, there are a number of reputable cooking schools in Bologna that offer a selection of lessons. Plan ahead to learn about course times and availability.

Returning to Tagliatelle al Ragù, you will notice that the ragù is not minced-meat swimming-in-tomato sauce, which you may have eaten outside of Italy. Rather, the ragù starts with a base of butter, onions, carrots and celery. Add a touch of tomato sauce, some minced meat, and even pancetta (a type of bacon), and you are almost there. Every restaurant will serve a twist of their own family's recipe. We've heard from some restaurants that they also include prosciutto and mortadella into the meat mix. It's a hearty meal, or even a substantial first plate if you are really hungry.

You can find an official version of the recipe on the site of the Accademia Italiana Della Cucina[23].

We have a bit of fun using the price of Tagliatelle al Ragu as a general indicator of the costliness of a restaurant. 7-9 Euros for Tagliatelle is a reasonably-priced restaurant. 10-12 Euros for the dish is mid-range. If you see 13 Euros or more, you are entering into a high-priced restaurant, which may be trying to offer a more chic cuisine. Regardless of the price though, a good trattoria should not compromise on quality! If it is home-made, you shouldn't expect much of a difference in taste between a respectable restaurant that serves Tagliatelle for 9 Euros or one that charges 13 Euros. I tend to avoid fancy overpriced Italian restaurants because I believe that the beauty of the Italian cuisine is its basic ingredients, which are fresh and of good quality. Many Italian dishes are founded on hearty home-cooked recipes, and are not overly fancy. The menus or prices shouldn't be either.

So forget about spaghetti when you visit Bologna, and dig into a bowl of tagliatelle al ragù.

3.4
All in the name

I've been obsessing about the name and logo for the B&B over the past month. The opening date is 3 months away, and time is flying. Before opening, I still need to register the B&B with the city, sign-up and prepare the property profiles on the major reservation websites, and create the B&B's website, Facebook page, business cards and more. I can't complete any of these, without a name and logo.

I would like a name and logo that's original, represents Bologna, sounds and looks professional, and gives potential guests the impression that this isn't the typical Italian B&B. I'm not demanding much ;-). Unfortunately, I can't afford to hire an advertising and graphic design service. I'll need all the cash I have to complete the renovations and buy all the supplies. Having dabbled in very basic graphic and web design, I've decided to try it myself. The end result may look amateur, but it will need to be good enough, for now.

After trying all sorts of brainstorming, and scribbling down many ideas for the name, I keep coming back to one option. My friends have also been making the same suggestion. Maybe I'm resisting it because it seems too simple, obvious, and lazy. Although, it may actually work. The idea is to use my last name 'Benvenuto', which is the Italian word for 'welcome'. My friends tease me, saying that it's a fitting name, and maybe even fate. I think it could make a cute anecdote to share with guests.

'Benvenuto B&B' sounds too casual, so I've decided to modify it to 'il Benvenuto Bologna'. In Italian, you can say to someone 'benvenuto!' as a simple exclamation of welcome. Or, you can be more formal by saying 'le do il benvenuto', which means 'I welcome you'.

Feeling fairly certain that I've settled on the name, I've also been working to design the logo. I downloaded a 30 day free-demo version of a graphic design software, and have been playing with different ways to visualize the name.

I would like the logo to be uncomplicated, and also highlight Bologna's beautiful features. My ideas haven't worked out visually though. I've trashed most of the results, and am too embarrassed to show you what they looked like.

For example, I've been trying to incorporate an image of Bologna's two towers, known as 'le due torri'. They are two medieval towers that stand side by side, at the end of Via Rizzoli, a minute's walk from Piazza Maggiore. The tallest tower, known as the Torre Degli Asinelli was built in the 1100s, and is about 97 meters tall.

This tower captures your attention, as it can be clearly viewed as you walk down Via Ugo Bassi and Via Rizzoli. It's open to the public to visit, and the entrance costs only a few Euros. If you don't mind climbing 498 wooden steps, and have no problem with vertigo, visiting the tower is an absolute must! The 360 degree view of Bologna from the top terrace is impressive. You can spot all the major landmarks, city architecture, and even the hills behind Bologna. I also like spying on all the roof-top terraces that are visible from above. It's like seeing a different style of living that's hidden from the street-level view.

Bolognesi can be somewhat superstitious, and there is a superstition related to this tower. They believe that if a student climbs the tower before they have finished their studies, they will not graduate. Apparently, many university students will avoid the climb before graduation.

The second tower just beside the Torre Degli Asinelli is called the Torre Garisenda. It currently stands at about 47 meters, but is said to have originally reached 60 meters. After it was built, the ground beneath this tower began to give-in, and the tower started to lean. Because of the danger it was posing, it's height was lowered during the 14th century. They say that Dante had seen this tower leaning in its original height, and referenced it in his work 'Inferno', in the 31st Canto. It actually leans at a dramatic angle, but capturing the angle in a foto is illusive. We keep trying from different positions, and sometimes it even comes out looking straight.

When bringing friends and relatives to see the two towers, we are usually asked if these are the only towers in Bologna. While their prominence and position draw people's attention, they aren't the only towers. Bologna is known as the town of towers, and in Italian is even referred to as 'la turrita'. Originally, there were around 100 towers built during the 12th century. Today, there are still <u>24 towers</u>[24] standing. The towers were built for military purposes, and also to display family status. The more important and wealthy you were, the bigger the tower you built. Maybe it's a male obsession. You can actually see the tops of a couple of other towers from Piazza Maggiore. Once you discover some other towers, you suddenly start noticing more popping-up in the background as you walk around Bologna.

Unfortunately, I haven't managed to fit the two towers in the logo. I've tried superimposing edited images in many different ways, and I even sketched the towers, but nothing looks right.

So, instead of focusing on the towers as a primary image, I've being playing with the shape of the letter 'B'. The letter repeats itself in the name, and its shape, rotated in different ways could resemble a number of things, even a bed, depending on the font.

Accidentally, while playing with different ways to distort the outline of the 'B', I've ended up with an interesting result. The 'B' now looks like this image.

The arches of the upper part of the 'B' remind me of Bologna's 'portici', or arcades. The city is also known for its network of portici, which protect almost 40 kilometres[25] of sidewalk. Their forms, shapes and material vary, representing different historical periods of the city. The scenery is picturesque, and you can spend hours exploring all the portici. They are also very practical, as they shade you from the hot summer sun, and give you cover from the rain.

The frescos decorating the portici on the west corner of Via Farini and Piazza Cavour are some of my favourite. They are beautiful during the day, and even more stunning when lit-up at night. They surround the Banca D'Italia (Bank of Italy) palazzo, and were painted by Gaetano Lodi[26], an artist of the 1800s. Each section represents an historical fact related to the history of Italy.

If you are on Via dell'Indipendenza, under the portici at the corner where it meets Via Rizzoli, look up. You will find more frescos decorating the portici. There is also writing in the centre of each portici, which together reads '***Panis vita, canabis protectio, vinum laetitia***'. This means 'bread is life, cannabis is protection, and wine is happiness.' The middle part apparently references the wealth that Bologna accumulated from the cultivation of hemp. Maybe that's where some of its reputation for being the more liberal Italian city comes from.

One of Bologna's most know walks under the portici, is the hike to the Santuario della Madonna di San Luca. The entire 3.8 km route up to San Luca is protected by the longest stretch of portici in the world. Start walking from Porta Saragozza along Via Saragozza, and never stray from the portici. You will eventually reach the Arco Meloncello e Portico di San Luca, a large portico that signals the start of the climb up the hill to San Luca.

Keep on following the portici until you reach San Luca. There are 664 portici from Porta Saragozza to San Luca. Once a year, the Catholic church organizes a procession to walk the icon of the Virgin Mary from San Luca down into the city, where she stays for a week of festivities. Originally, the faithful would make the route on their knees, in prayer. Nowadays, the Bolognesi like to make it their weekend fitness hike, either by foot, running, or even by bike on the road beside. Our friends have cautioned us that walking up together as a couple is considered bad luck, and can lead to a broken relationship. Some still avoid making the walk with their significant other.   Bologna seems to have plenty of superstitions. We aren't superstitious though ;-).

Considering their architectural and historical relevance, as well as their beauty, featuring the portici in the logo seems fitting. I've coloured the arches of the 'B' in a yellow-ochre. This is one of the dominant colours of the portici that one sees when walking through Bologna, along with red, from the brinks and many facades.

I've also added blue colouring inside the bottom part of the 'B' to highlight Bologna's canals. While there is only one canal that is still visible, it has special meaning for me, as I described in my chapter 'Bologna – a city of water?'

Combining both the name and the image, I've created the design below. If you look closely at the word 'il' sitting in the first arch, you will note that the smaller 'i' is leaning on an angle beside the tall 'l'. It's my homage of the two towers. You can find a colour version of this logo on the back cover of this book.

il Benvenuto

BED & BREAKFAST
BOLOGNA

Now I can get started on designing the website!

3.5
A step back in time

I've recently discovered one of the most enchanting spaces that I've ever visited, and it's in Bologna.

I need to thank my social network again, and specifically Domenico. He sent me a link to a guided tour that was being organized by a cultural association called Didasco[27]. For a small annual membership fee, one can take part in a variety of different cultural and historic tours in and around Bologna. There is a small fee to participate in each tour, and the guides are passionate, who have researched the stories behind the tour, to make the experience as alive and authentic as possible.

We shared the details of the tour with other friends, and in the end, there were about ten of us who met at the designated starting point. There, we joined a larger group of about thirty other enthusiastic Bolognesi, and waited for the tour to start. I really admire how Italians appreciate their history and culture. They are always eager to visit a museum, historic site, art gallery and new exhibit.

It was an outdoor night tour, starting at 9:00pm. The topic was speed - the automotive industry, and the venue was the Certosa di Bologna, Cimitero Storico Monumentale[28]. Translated, it's the Historic Monumental Cemetery, and Carthusian Monastery of Bologna.

While the topic of the tour was interesting, the real star of that night was the cemetery, which I'll refer to as the Certosa for short.

It was absolutely impressive. I was left stunned walking its courtyards and halls, trying to absorb all the sensations from hundreds of years of history.

Why isn't this cemetery described as a **must see** on all tourism websites and guides?

I learned that in the 1800s, the Certosa was a popular venue to visit and pass the day. It was even a destination for known intellectuals like Lord Byron and Charles Dickens.

What a brilliant idea to organize the tour at night. This was an opportunity to see the cemetery in a different setting, as it's only open to the public during the daytime. It was my first time ever visiting the Certosa, and walking around at night was enchanting. There aren't any lampposts in the cemetery, and we were guided by lawn torches and candles. I was able to catch glimpses of grandiose halls hidden in darkness, and majestic monuments marking tombs, as we walked along the tour path. I will definite return during the daytime to explore on my own.

The tour guide led us around, describing the stories of various tombstones and monuments related to the region's automotive history, including the tombs of famous people like Alfieri Maserati[29], founder of Maserati.

She was also proud of the accomplishments of the Certosa, and described some of its general history, like how it is three years older than the cemetery Père-Lachaise in Paris. The Certosa was designated as a cemetery in 1801, and was one of the first 'extra-urbana' cemeteries in Europe, a cemetery that was located outside the main town. Before, cemeteries were usually co-located beside their churches. In 1804, Napoleon Bonaparte issued a decree for the creation of cemeteries outside town centres, as places for everyone to be buried, regardless of religion or beliefs. Père-Lachaise opened in 1804. Bologna however, was ahead of the game.

The guide was adamant about preventing people from taking fotos. This was extremely frustrating. Between the soft glow of the moonlight, the orange embers from the torches, and the shadows dancing around the monuments, we were all itching to capture the atmosphere and the beauty by foto.

I couldn't understand why fotos weren't allowed. It's a public cemetery. The guide had previously described how a low level of awareness of the Certosa has led to minimal interest and support for the cemetery. As a result, some parts are in serious deterioration. While this state of ruin adds to the atmosphere of stepping back in time, renewed interest can help bring the investment needed to preserve the art and architecture that span hundreds of years. Some social marketing to demonstrate its beauty could really help draw visitors back to the Certosa.

I discovered later from a friend, who works in the government for the restoration of historic buildings and monuments, that the Certosa is considered a property of the city, as well as a museum, and consequently fotos aren't allowed. That still doesn't answer my question of **why** fotos are forbidden. Regardless, he explained that a person can submit a special request to the mayor to request approval to take fotos.

I was grateful to Domenico for introducing me to the Certosa, and couldn't stop talking about the tour to José afterwards.

José and I arranged to return to the Certosa during the daytime, to explore the cemetery at our own pace.

From the Certosa's main entrance courtyard, if you make your way to the campuses to the right, you will find large outdoor spaces with tombstones typical of a modern European cemetery.

Instead, walk straight through the courtyard, and then to the open campus to the left. You will reach another outdoor campus with older tombs starting from the early 1900s. Here you will find a number of tombs that embody the liberty style or art nouveau of the early 1900s.

I also discovered the haunting memorial to the fallen Partigiani, the Italian rebels who resisted against the fascists during the Second World War. In keeping with the strange rule of no fotos, I haven't included any fotos directly in this chapter, even though I may have taken a few during my last visit ;-). You can however preview this memorial by visiting the following site of the City of Bologna:

- http://www.storiaememoriadibologna.it/monumento-ossario-ai-caduti-partigiani-1019-opera

I find this area of the cemetery very peaceful, with beautiful sculptures and statues that rest in honour of the tombs they protect.

To catch a glimpse of some of the exquisite art waiting to be rediscovered at the Certosa, visit the following link:

- http://www.storiaememoriadibologna.it/la-certosa-un-luogo-rappresentativo-di-stili-e-art-840-evento

The part of the Certosa that I find absolutely exquisite is the actual Certosa complex - the former Carthusian monastery. While the cemetery opened in 1801, the actual monastery was started in 1334. The monastery thrived for hundreds of years, until it was closed by Napoleon in 1796, as part of his efforts to suppress religious organizations across his territories. Interestingly, Napoleon's sister Elisa was buried in Bologna. Her tomb is in the Basilica San Petronio, located in Piazza Maggiore.

In the old Certosa complex, you can walk the grand corridors and contemplate the tombs, which have been placed everywhere, along the floors, walls and even underground levels. It's impossible to avoid walking over tombs, as almost all the available space has been taken to house the dead. There is a special contrast between the large gallery spaces and the silent commemoration of the many tombs, which leaves many people in a state of contemplation. This link offers some fotos of one of the galleries, Galleria degli Angeli:

- http://www.storiaememoriadibologna.it/galleria-degli-angeli-chiostro-vii-galleria-tre-na-1976-luogo

The older tombs are also located in the Certosa complex. You may note that many of the tombs dating before the mid 1800s were decorated by works of art in stucco and frescos, instead of marble. The reason is that it wasn't until after the mid 1800s, when the train system was developed, that heavy materials like marble and bronze could be easily transported to Bologna.

I've discovered some of my favourite sculptures in the Certosa. The delicate sculpting of the veiled face of the statue following this link is breathtaking:

- http://www.storiaememoriadibologna.it/monumento-fornasari-1199-opera

Also, the statue in this other link of a woman kneeling in silent sadness is captivating and makes you wonder about the grave she is watching over:

- http://www.storiaememoriadibologna.it/monumento-ropa-1197-opera

After walking around Bologna's Certosa, I've come to appreciate the relationship of using art to honour the dead. It's a shame to see that these traditions have been forgotten.

We spent a good three hours exploring the Certosa during the daytime, and realized that we still missed many of the hidden halls and spaces, and will need to return to continue our exploration. I definitely plan on suggesting a visit of the Certosa to future guests who decide to stay in town for a few days.

3.6
Sound-proofing or dumb-proofing?

As much as you try to anticipate all the things you need to make your perfect B&B, there will always be a moment where your brain takes a pause, leaving you with a stupid and costly mistake to correct.

I spent a few years travelling every week for work, and whether I stayed in a fancy 4 or 5 star hotel, or a simpler Bed and Breakfast, one of the things that would really irritate me was having to listen to all the noise from the people staying in the adjacent rooms, or moving through the hallways.

Since the initial blueprint discussions, I advised Domenico, my Architetto, that it was really important to make the rooms as sound-proofed as possible, within my budget of course. Guests should be able to have a good night's sleep, or even an undisturbed siesta.

So we designed a couple of solutions into the renovation. The first is to invest in sound-proofed bedroom doors, with features like a 'guillotine', which descends from the bottom of the door to the floor, when you close the door.

The second is to increase the width and insulation of the walls, which separate the rooms from each other, as well as from the hallway. For additional effect, we also plan to mount a double layer of drywall on these walls.

We thought we had everything covered.

During one of my visits to the apartment to see the progress of the renovations, Raffaele, the manager from the renovation company was there speaking with his workers. He saw me enter, and waved, indicating that he wanted to speak with me. Raffaele is a fantastic renovation manager. Under his watch, the work is progressing speedily. His eye for quality is fantastic, and he seems genuinely concerned to make the B&B renovations the best possible. He and his team are also proactive in identifying potential issues.

Generally though, when he wants to speak with me about an issue, it eventually means that there will be an extra cost. It almost always involves work not defined in the original Computo Metrico and quote.

The renovations have reached the stage where the new electrical and plumbing installations have been laid out, and the frames of the new walls are up. The plumber was on-site, installing some of the plumbing components for the bathrooms.

Raffaele approached me, and after our usual salutations of 'ciao, come va', he mentioned that he thought there is an issue with the toilets. He brought me to one of the rooms and pointed to the toilet's water flushing container that the plumber was installing in the wall.

When Domenico and I went searching for the bathroom fixtures, I selected a toilet model where only the toilet seat/bowl is visible in the bathroom. The container that fills-up and discharges the water is installed in the wall, so a person only sees the buttons to flush the water. Domenico recommended this product, explaining that that toilets look modern, would be simple to keep clean, and would take up less space in the bathrooms.

'Per the blueprints, this container is being installed in the wall that separates the bathroom of one bedroom from a different bedroom', Raffaele explained. 'Even after placing the insulation in the walls, as well as the double layer of drywall for sound-proofing, there isn't enough space between the container and the wall to place enough insulation to make it sound-proofed. Every time a guest flushes their toilet, the guests in the adjacent room will hear it, clearly.'

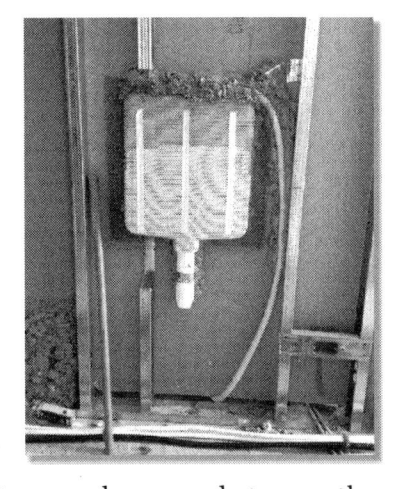

Shit! And no one caught this before? I felt the urge to immediately blame Domenico. He's the expert. I had repeated since the start that sound-proofing was important, and he should have foreseen it. However, I had also completely missed it.

'Focus on the solution, not the problem', I thought. Hopefully Raffaele and the plumber already have a solution in mind that won't involve having to buy three new toilets, as this would be a problem for three out of the four rooms.

'Is there anything we can do to fix this?' I asked Raffaele.

'Possibly. There is a type of insulating material that is about a centimetre thick. We could try to place a couple of layers between the container and wall. It should reduce the noise of the flushing water, but it won't eliminate it completely. We should also cover the pipes and even the boxes of the electrical outlets with this material. The material is expensive though.'

'How expensive?' I asked.

'We wouldn't need a lot, but it will cost at least a few hundred Euros', Raffaele informed me.

'Is there any other alternative?'

'Other than buying new toilets, we don't think so. Also, things like electrical outlets and light switches, which interrupt the barrier of the walls, will also reduce the sound-proofing of the walls. This material can really help, if sound-proofing is important for you.'

'Ok. Let's get the material then.'

A few days later, I received the work variance email from the renovation company, requesting approval to proceed with the purchase and installation of the insulation material.

It's going to cost me an extra 860.60 Euros. I seem to be gritting my teeth a lot lately. I printed, signed, scanned, and emailed back the form to the company.

The unplanned costs continue to increase, and I hope that I will be able to stay within budget.

Some lessons are costly.

3.7
The scavenger hunt

'What do you mean you don't know where the lights that I've ordered are?' I tried not to raise my voice, incredulously. 'I placed the order over three months ago, and I've been waiting patiently. You were the ones that called me yesterday to say that my order arrived. So here I am!'

'We received only 3 lights,' the employee from the lighting department of the major electronics store replied.

'My order is for 13 lights,' I repeated, pointing to my copy of the invoice. 'Look, the renovations of my B&B are almost complete, and we will be opening in a month. The missing lights are for the main hallway, and for all the showers. I can't open the B&B with wires hanging from the walls and ceilings. I need those lights. Can you call the supplier to find out what's happening?'

'I will try to call them now,' the employee responded, and went to the back office to make the call.

WTF! Now I was pissed. These lights aren't cheap. In fact, they're considered higher-end design lights, and each one costs about 170 Euros.

Would you pay 170 Euros for a small light fixture?

I normally wouldn't. However, they were the only ones I could find in Bologna. Domenico and I visited all types of stores, in search of the light fixtures for the B&B. It was like an impossible scavenger hunt, and I had become desperate to find nice pieces that wouldn't burst my budget.

The idea for the shower and hallway lights was simple. For the showers, I was looking for modern, cylindrical lights that could be installed flush to the ceiling. For the hallway walls, I wanted the same cylindrical look, with light emanating from both the top and bottom of the cylinders. I wanted the light to accentuate the 3-meter high ceilings, and also shine light down on future paintings, which I planned to find and hang along the walls of the hallway, to create a mini art gallery.

I had searched all the small lighting shops around Bologna, as well the larger home construction chain stores like Leroy Merlin and Brico. I don't even want to mention Ikea. I feel like a piece of Ikea furniture, after visiting it almost every week for the last few months, in search of all sorts of supplies. After all the hunting though, I hadn't found the right lights.

Domenico repeated that the only option was the lighting department of this electronic store. They offer a wide selection of fixtures that are 'design', which can be ordered directly from the different manufacturers' catalogues. Domenico enjoyed scanning the catalogues, and pointing out modern sleek fixtures from top Italian manufactures.

Italians love 'design'. We've visited many homes of friends that proudly display decorative design pieces, like a Kartell table lamp. If you pay attention, you may spot a Kartell lamp almost everywhere.

'Design' however, comes with a **much** higher price tag.

I think I'm spoiled from all the store options available in a city like Toronto. There, I'm sure I could have found what I was looking even at a Home Depot, and not be forced to spend a crazy amount.

In Italy, except for Ikea, stores with reasonably priced products are rare.

Eventually I relented, and placed an order for designer lights out of a catalogue. The price was almost 1,950 Euros for 4 shower ceiling lights, 3 hallway ceiling lights, and 6 hallway wall lights.

Now, after waiting months for these designer lights to arrive, they are nowhere to be found.

The employee finally returned. 'It seems like the order for the hallway wall lights and the shower ceiling lights was never made. If you like, we can place a new order,' she offered.

'Really? You must be joking. I can't wait another 3 months for lights that may or may not arrive!'

Just breathe. Maybe this was one of those 'blessing in disguise' moments. I had always felt ripped-off by the price, and was never fully convinced that it was my only option. Then I had a thought...

'You know what' I said to the employee, 'I'll just take the 3 lights that arrived. You can cancel the rest of the order.'

I paid for the lights and left the store, brimming still from the anger and adrenaline, but also energized by my idea.

I was heading to Switzerland in a few days for work meetings, and would stay the weekend there with José. There are some interesting home design stores not too far from where José lives, and maybe I'll be able to find the lights there!

On the Saturday in Switzerland, we went out to do some store hopping. After just a couple of stores, we found the lights for the hallway walls. The model was exactly what I was looking for. It was a sleek, silver cylinder, with light that comes out from the top and bottom of the cylinder. Did I mention that they only cost 50 Euros each?

The shower lights were more challenging. The Elettricista (electrician) had advised me that the fixtures need to meet a certain industry standard for waterproofing. Even though they were being installed against the ceiling, 3 meters up, and well above the showerheads, the Elettricista said it was better to be cautious.

The lights we had seen were either extremely kitsch, with features like multi-coloured LED, or they were pot-lights, which would be impossible to install in the ceilings of the apartment.

After a few circles around the indoor lighting section of a large home renovation store, I thought maybe I needed to think differently. Instead of looking for *internal* home or bath fixtures, maybe I should focus on the section for **external** home lights. At a minimum, external lights would need to meet the waterproofing standard, to be protected from the weather.

Jackpot! There, in the section for external lighting, I found the fixtures I was looking for. Modern cylindrical lights that cost only 50 Euros each, instead of the 170 Euro designer lights I had previously ordered. The design was almost identical!

I was definitely satisfied after that trip to Switzerland :-).

3.8
Where did all the money go?

No matter how closely I've tried to control my budget, it looks like I'll be going over budget.

I have totalled the remaining renovation invoices to pay, including all the unplanned variations, and I've finally completed an estimation of the costs of all the furnishings and supplies that will be needed to start the B&B, and there is no doubt, I will be short of cash.

Admittedly, I never really thought that the cost for the B&B furnishings and supplies would be so high, but now that I have listed and researched each item, reality has hit me. With 4 bedrooms and bathrooms, as well as breakfast to arrange, my list has grown tremendously. Let's see...bases and headboards for the beds, mattresses, night-tables, table lamps, mirrors, sheets, duvets, pillows, towels, mini-fridges, TVs, bistro tables and chairs, dishes, cutlery...and the list goes on.

I will need a loan to have the cash flow necessary to be ready for opening day.

So here I am at my bank, speaking with my Representative about a loan.

It's not the same bank that provided me the mortgage I needed to buy the apartment, though. It's the bank where I created my first checking account, back when I arrived in Italy, and where my monthly pay-check is deposited.

I would highly recommend to any foreigner setting up home in Italy, to have accounts in multiple banks. If one bank doesn't offer a particular service or declines your request, you can quickly refer to your alternate bank, with which you already have a relationship. I did visit the bank that provided my mortgage, but they were quick to say they did not provide the type of loan I was looking for, and that the loan they could offer would be costly. My other bank, however, seems more interested to offer a loan.

Another reason to have accounts in multiple banks is easier access to your money. In Europe, especially in Italy, there are many controls aimed at preventing fraud, money laundering, and other tax evasion. For example, big transactions are registered and monitored. Small money transactions are also limited. You will likely have daily, weekly, and monthly domestic ATM withdrawal limits. You may also find tougher restrictions for ATM and in-store payments conducted outside the country, even if you are still in Europe.

During my first two years in Italy, I travelled out of Italy weekly for work. There were a number of times where I would be at a hotel or train station, and not be able to pay because I had reached a limit. I would then get on the phone, desperately trying to contact my bank, to have them unblock my account so I could access my money.

You can, and should request a credit card, as it will give you some additional freedom. But you will not have as much freedom as you may expect, especially if you are used to North American credit cards. A credit card where you are obligated to pay only a minimum monthly sum, is much harder to obtain in Italy. The credit cards normally offered in Italy have a low monthly limit, usually only a couple thousand Euros, and require full payment at the end of the month. If you spend let's say 1,500 Euros during one month, at the end of the month the total 1,500 Euros will be automatically taken from your bank account. Your bank account is directly linked, to facilitate the monthly payment of the **full** balance on your card.

I actually think that this is a better approach. It means that people learn to have more control over their spending, and they are disciplined in spending only what they earn. As a result, I do not know many Italians who are stuck paying off endless personal debt. Debt is viewed negatively, and Italians try to avoid it as much as possible.

How do people manage to pay for things like vacations, and other larger purchases? There is usually a savings program built into your pay-check. Many companies in Europe provide their employees with a *monthly* pay-check. However, a portion of the total annual salary is withheld so that you get a 13th payment, usually in December. People look forward to their double pay-check in December. It's not unusual in some countries, like Spain, to also arrange a 14th pay-check. Let me bust the mythology around this though. The 13th or 14th pay-check is **not an addition to your salary** – it's not a bonus. Your annual salary is set in your contract. So for example, if your annual salary is 50,000 Euros, instead of receiving the 50,000 in 12 instalments throughout the year, you will receive it in 13 or 14 payments. In the end, it's still the same annual salary amount.

Overall, this discipline on personal finances can create challenges though. For example, if you are in the process of doing a large project, say a renovation, you will need to pay much more attention to your cash flow, and have alternate cash flow options available.

So here I am at my bank, looking for an alternative. My bank Representative printed and handed me the loan application.

'I need you to sign here on this page, and then here, and here, here and here, and here and here...' My god - I'm always entertained at how many signatures you are asked for in a single document. I got busy signing.

'Once your request is processed, we will contact you to let you know the result,' the Representative advised me.

A week later she called to say that the loan was approved.

It's time to finish the B&B!

4 Learning to Operate a Bed & Breakfast

4.1
Where's the party?

Cultivating relationships makes life so much richer in Italy, and also helps you get things done.

I've reached out to friends countless times to ask for advice on how things work in Italy, or to ask if they have reliable contacts. My starting point when I need to do something is almost always my social network. You never know if a friend knows someone, who knows someone, who knows someone... you get the picture.

The only reason we've been able to renovate and prepare the Bed and Breakfast so quickly, is that we've had the support of some really good friends.

As a way to thank everyone involved, and also to create some awareness and excitement for the Bed and Breakfast, we decided to host an Inauguration party. Oh and what a party. We definitely learned what to do, and what not to do, if we ever want to host another party again. The Inauguration party was the follow-up to the smaller Demolition party I had organized before the start of the renovations.

A party in Italy isn't a party if it doesn't have: an engaging theme, good wine and bolle (slang for some bubbly or prosecco), creative decorations, food and more food, great friends, and some fotos to share, tag on Facebook and laugh about afterwards.

Oh, and did I forget to mention 'drama'? A good party always needs a touch of drama!

We opened the Bed and Breakfast in mid-September 2014, jumping right into the fire during one of Bologna's busiest international trade fairs. We were so occupied with getting the B&B ready, and figuring out how to actually run the B&B without drowning, that we decided to wait to host the Inauguration party until October.

I tend to over-think when it comes to themes, and after mashing around ideas over and over again, we finally thought - what better theme for an October party than Halloween? The 31st fell on a Friday, which was perfect for an evening party. Saturdays are coveted in Italy, with most people preferring to keep their Saturdays free for personal engagements. I could also capitalize on my North American origin, and offer a more authentic Halloween experience. While Italians enjoy the masquerade-themed Carnevale in February, Halloween hasn't really been adopted in Italy. It's considered an activity more for children, and many adults are not familiar with the traditions.

The theme was set. Now we needed Halloween decorations. This called for a scavenger hunt around town. We visited plenty of dollar stores, as they each stocked a limited selection of Halloween gadgets. There we found the typical spider webbing that could be hung around the house. We also found some great traditional candles in red plastic covers, which are usually used in cemeteries in Italy. In a fabric shop down our street, we purchase a few meters of black cloth to use as table coverings. Also, during a trip to the hardware store, we found some styrofoam that could be transformed into tombstones. The plan was to decorate the kitchen / living room area like a haunted house, and to create a cemetery in the entrance hallway of the B&B. Pumpkins seemed to be a problem. The local grocery stores only stocked a couple of pumpkins, but they weren't fresh and wouldn't last until the 31st. It took a number of visits to find a few pumpkins that were good enough. It isn't Halloween without jack o'lanterns.

While the decorations were coming together, it felt like something was still missing. That was until one afternoon, while strolling around town, we passed a small private art gallery about a five minute walk from our home. Hanging in the window were a couple of large paintings depicting macabre monsters. One painting was of a silhouette of a monster hidden in mist, like a creature out of an Aliens film. The other was a devilish face painted in fire-red on a black background. They were absolutely fantastic.

I didn't have money to buy original art, but just maybe the artist would be willing to lend a piece or two??? It was worth a try, wasn't it? José was doubtful, but I dragged him into the gallery.

The space inside was small, and all the walls were covered with original art in different styles. There were renaissance-style portraits, contemporary city-scapes, and still-life so life-like you could reach out and grab the vegetables. A woman who was attending the gallery asked if we had any questions. We started to speak about the pieces, and learned that she was the artist, and that all the pieces displayed were her work. Her name is Ornella Stingo[30] and she welcomed us to her gallery. Wow! She was like a painting chameleon, so skilled that she could paint in any style.

We introduced ourselves and explained that we run a Bed and Breakfast nearby. Then came the sales pitch. We were hosting our Inauguration party with a Halloween theme, and her amazing paintings would make the scene complete. Was there any chance she could lend us the paintings for the night of the 31st? She seemed sceptical, but at least she didn't reply with an immediate 'no'. This meant that there was a chance! We were of course complete strangers, and it was natural for her to be hesitant.

We continued to chat and gave her our business card with our website and Facebook page. We also invited her to the Inauguration. Ornella liked the Halloween theme. However, the two paintings in the front window were there to attract customers, and she didn't want to leave her display empty. She did mention then that she had other paintings that she may be able to lend us, if we were willing to sign a waiver accepting responsibility for possible damages. Are you kidding? Of course!!!

She took us downstairs to the basement, where the walls were also covered from floor to ceiling with other amazing work. From a backroom she retrieved three very large canvasses that were rolled up. One by one, she unrolled them to display her work. Two were oil paintings of skulls, painted in different styles. The third was a painting of Hamlet with a skull. However, unlike the typical interpretation where you would find Hamlet contemplating the skull in his hand, her version had the skull dressed like a reaper, holding Hamlet's head in its hand. I could already visualize which wall would feature which painting, and told Ornella that they were absolutely perfect!

With the decorations set, we still needed a photographer, and to organize the food and wine. The photographer we solved quickly, while out one night with friends at a local bar. There was a bar that organized a Friday evening aperitivo with a great buffet once a month. Like other good events, there would always be a young photographer taking pictures of the participants. A few days later you would find your pictures posted on their Facebook page, which you can tag or share with friends.

That night we started a conversation with the photographer, a young Italian, who had an eye for capturing close-ups of the social scene. Photographing parties was his moonlighting gig. We mentioned our party and agreed to call him to arrange a visit of the B&B, so that he could see the space and we could agree on a price. The price ended up being very reasonable, and he even offered to do some editing. The photographer was booked!

The food was the easiest to organize. We decided to create a buffet with finger foods, including sliced prosciutto, cheeses, salads and more.

I would also prepare some of my specialty sweets that were becoming well known, like a New York style Cheesecake.

The wine was worrying me though. Italians are more knowledgeable of the different types of Italian wines, and are quick in selecting quality wines based on the variety and region. They are also quick to criticize a poor wine. One of the most common reasons I've heard of why friends won't frequent a bar, is a poor wine selection. A good wine selection at a good price can even be more important than the quality of service or cleanliness of the bar.

I mentioned the topic of finding the right wine every time we met up with different friends. Finally, Domenica, one of the first friends I made in Bologna, suggested that I speak with a friend of ours who works in a boutique shoe store. She reminded me that he organizes an aperitivo at least once a year for the store, and maybe he could recommend his supplier. That was a great lead! I called him and posed the question. He recommended that I call his supplier, Michele Carusi, who had a selection of quality wines for various budgets, and he was reliable.

After a conversation with Michele, he invited us to visit his family's enoteca Carusi[31], which they have been running for more than 40 years (enoteca refers to a wine store, bar or cellar). The shop is located in

Bolognina, a neighbourhood that flourished during an industrial boom in the first half of the 20th century. The enoteca is just outside Bologna's centre, in Via Matteotti, a main road that extends perpendicular from the circular ring-road that surrounds Bologna's centre.

When we arrived, we found two elderly men behind the cash register. The store itself featured display cases full of different assortments of wrapped candies and chocolates. There wasn't much wine on display. Were we at the right place?

We asked for Michele, and one of the men replied that he should be arriving shortly. After a few minutes, Michele entered the store. He greeted us warmly and invited us to the basement. Walking down the stairs, we entered a large showroom with wall-to-wall shelving filled with many varieties of Italian wines. One would never know of the fantastic wine selection below, if you were just passing by the store on the street level.

Michele began by asking us what types of wines we would like. We wanted to offer our guests an option of a red wine, a white wine and a prosecco. The current fashion in Bologna is to drink white wine or prosecco for aperitivo, and we knew that we needed to buy greater quantities of the white wine and prosecco. Domenica had recommended that we buy at least one bottle per person, which sounded like an exaggeration. On the other hand, I do repeatedly describe how some of our friends can drink like fish!

Michele asked us about our preferences, and we replied that we were too inexperienced to select the right wine. Instead, we settled on our ideal price range, and he described some of the vintages that his clients preferred. José and I had decided earlier to let the experts choose. Our plan was to buy different samples, and invite our friends over for a small degustazione - a wine tasting.

After sending out a quick invitation to our friends, and preparing a selection of salumi e formaggi, we had a great evening hosting friends, who also selected the perfect wines for us.

We let Michele know which wines were selected and the quantities of each that we wanted. He even offered to lend us wine glasses, and to deliver the wine and glasses the day of the party. We couldn't be any more grateful!

We were almost ready for the party. All that was left was a touch of drama.

I had decided to prepare and send the invitation via Facebook. It's an easy way to forward the invite to friends and to track RSVPs. Italians are also very savvy with social marking and almost everyone has a Facebook profile.

Unfortunately, getting people to commit isn't easy. In Italy, when it comes to RSVPing, people can generally fall into one of the following categories.

Faithful: These are the ones who will say they will attend, and will actually make it! Unfortunately, they are rare.

Flabbergasted: How can you possibly ask these people to commit when the date is so far away? Anything can happen between now and the party, and it's unreasonable to expect an answer. My theory is that there is also a subset in this group who wait to see if there is a better offer. There are a lot of people that fall into this group. Plan to send out reminders. You will likely receive their answer only a day or two before the party.

Magari: This is one of Italian's most beautiful words, and most frustrating. It has many meanings depending on the context, and is usually inserted casually into a phrase or conversation. Don't be fooled though. When it is said, it is more deliberate than you think. In a sentence, magari can be similar to the expressions 'I wish!' or 'it's possible', or in the case of an RSVP response 'maybe'. For example, you may hear a sentence like "magari, if I get off of work on time, I will come to the party. Be forewarned. Our experience to date is that when someone slips in the word 'magari', they will likely be a 99% no-show.

Gregarious: These are your friends who, a day or two before the party, will give you a quick call or send a WhatsApp, asking if it's ok to bring along a friend or two, whom you may not know. I actually like this group. It is a great way to make new friends. I've also benefited from being one of those people who have tagged along! These surprise guests help compensate for any no-shows.

One final group, and it's a group that we naively did not anticipate, is the **party-crashers**. These are the ones that obtain the invite somehow, do not RSVP and show-up at the door. Remember how I said that Italians are savvy with social marketing and Facebook? We learned that night that if you don't want the invitation to be open to this group, do not send the invitation via Facebook. Next time, we will only send private invitations via WhatsApp!

Luckily we only had around six party-crashers. Five were harmless. They were the first to show up. They grabbed a spot on our couch, and ate and drank all night. They, conversed with us and the other guests, but never introduced their names or who they were. We originally thought that they were friends of friends - part of the Gregarious group. However, after asking around, we finally realized that no one knew them.

The fifth party-crasher grabbed our attention when a couple we knew came to speak with us. This party-crasher was a handsome Italian, probably in his early thirties, with wavy dark hair and a smart outfit. He spent the early evening mingling politely with guests. Our friends asked us if we knew him, and after replying no, they told us that they had a store, and had video and fotos of him stealing. That wasn't good. We immediately asked some friends to stand guard by the laundry room, where we had set up the coat check. We also spread the word around to keep watch for him in case of pick-pocketing. After a half hour, our friends came to let us know that they had taken care of the situation. They approached the man, advised him that they had proof of him stealing, and suggested that it would be best for him to leave. They then guided him out the door.

Now, back to hosting the party and making sure that the buffet was replenished and glasses refilled. The party seemed to be going great, and everyone was enjoying themselves. People were exploring the Bed and Breakfast, mingling, and commenting on the costumes. Even the artist Ornella arrived with her husband, impressing the other guests with some creative make-up. Below is a foto of Ornella in her make-up.

The photographer was also doing his rounds snapping fotos of everyone. In the end, we counted over eighty guests who attended, and I was starting to think that a Halloween party was going to turn into an annual tradition.

A couple of the party-crashers asked if they could invite some additional friends. At this point, we thought why not. Around 11 pm, after the party-crashers themselves left, a group of around five people in their forties knocked on the door. We invited them in. By that point, the party was still going strong, with about twenty of our friends. This included a mix of straight and gay friends in various costumes. The group took a look inside, looked at each other, and turned around and left. A friend of ours, who was smoking outside the building entrance downstairs, said that as the group was exiting the building, they asked him if he knew if there was another party nearby that was less 'gay'.

Incredible... and they were the ones looking to crash a party with free food and drinks!

The guests were satisfied and there was enough food and wine for all. Everyone also loved the B&B, and were ready to spread the word. We couldn't have been happier with the outcome. At least no one reported a theft. Well, except for a friend who had tied his bike on the street, but found the lock broken and his bike stolen.

4.2
Bologna the hidden

'We weren't sure what to expect, but now that we've seen Bologna, we love the city!' Our guests from North America were excited to describe their previous day, as we served them breakfast. They were a mature couple who had visited Italy before, but had never been to Bologna.

After being open a few months, we've started to hear this opinion a lot.

'It's a shame that we only booked for a night. We'd like to come back and stay at least couple of nights to visit what we've missed.'

It's also not the first time that we've heard guests make this statement. It may sound like a tacky infomercial, or maybe the guests are just being polite and don't want to say something negative about the city we call home, but they seem genuine and enthusiastic when they talk about their visit.

Bologna's airport has been attracting a greater number of short-haul flights from across Europe, making the city more accessible. Even though it's not the traditional target destination for an Italian tour, it's a convenient entry point. From Bologna on the high speed train, you can reach Firenze in 34 minutes, Milano in 58 minutes, Venezia in 1 hour and 25 minutes, and even Roma in 1 hour and 54 minutes. The city is now finding itself hosting more and more visitors.

However, because it's an entry or departure point, the majority of our guests book for one night, either at the start of their trip, or at the end. They get a great introduction, but realize one night isn't enough.

There are tourists who do stay longer. They are the ones who have already visited the main destinations in Italy, and want to explore the regional cultures and flavours. Bologna is a great hub for them. Either by car or by regional train, they can arrange day trips to places like Ravenna - for the Byzantine mosaics, Modena - home of aceto balsamico (balsamic vinegar) and Luciano Pavarotti, and Parma – the epicentre of prosciutto.

'We have this travel guide from a renowned American travel author, and he discourages people from visiting Bologna in his guide,' our guests continued. 'Did you read it?'

'No I haven't' I replied (and I've also refrained from pointing out his name in this chapter).

The wife took out the guide, and indicates a very brief entry on Bologna where the author explains that Bologna isn't worth a stop.

'Really?' I was shocked. I may not have travelled as much as Mr. Steves, but my travelling shoes are quite worn, especially when it comes to touring Europe, and Italy.

'We're very happy that we came though,' they repeated.

'Maybe he didn't have a good host when he visited,' I offered. 'We should invite him to stay with us, and we can show him our adopted home.'

Bologna isn't a destination that hands you a standard tourist experience on a silver platter. It's a city that you explore and soak up the ambiance, as you wander through its historic streets, and interact with the locals.

Don't get me wrong, you can easily pass all your time visiting the main tourist sites in Bologna's centre. I've already described some of the more notable characteristics, like the medieval towers, 40 kilometres of portici, the hidden canal, and of course its vibrant social scene. The cuisine is also a delicious and necessary diversion, as it will give you a new appreciation for hand-made pasta. You won't look at dried pasta the same way again.

In Bologna, there is so much more to see than what's readily described in a tourist guide. Maybe the city isn't as savvy as it can be in advertising its hidden experiences. Sometimes though, a visit is more satisfying when you discover spots off the typical tourist track, and when a local introduces the sights that are special to them. Bologna has some fantastic discoveries.

One such hidden treasure is Santa Catarina, the patron saint of artists. Domenico, my Architetto, mentioned her one day, as we were walking through the neighbourhood just southwest of Piazza Maggiore. While you will likely find relics of saints in many churches you visit in Italy, Bologna offer's you a complete view of a saint, Santa Catarina. Her home is the small church called Santuario del Corpus Domini, located in Via Tagliapietre, about an 8 minute walk from Piazza Maggiore. The church was built in the late 1400s, but was damaged significantly in 1943 by bombing. You can see the extent of the damage by the patchworks of plaster along the walls and dome, which interrupt the scenes of the old frescos.

Santa Caterina isn't in the main part of the church. She waits patiently in an adjacent cappella. When entering the church, there is a door to the cappella on the left side. Walk through the door, and you will find la Santa sitting in her cappella, attended by a couple of nuns. She does have visiting hours[32] though, and can only be viewed during a few hours on certain days of the week.

Santa Caterina was born in 1413, and began her religious vocation at 13 years old. She died in 1463, and was buried, apparently directly in the earth, without a coffin[33]. Her fellow nuns, visiting her grave, noticed a sweet smell coming from the grave. The smell continued, and after 18 days, they exhumed her body, only to find her unspoiled. Her fame and following grew further, and she was brought back to the church, where you can find her sitting peacefully on a golden throne, encased in glass.

The cappella is beautifully decorated, and Santa Catarina, sitting on her throne, captures your attention in a fascinating and slightly morbid way. Some may find visiting her a bit uncomfortable, but when will you have a chance to meet a 600 year old saint? Taking pictures is forbidden, but if you would like a preview, do a quick Google search.

Another sight that we recommend to clients is San Michele in Bosco. A friend took me to visit San Michele one afternoon, a few months after I had moved to Bologna. While many tourist guides mention the 3.8 kilometre pilgrimage to San Luca, San Michele seems to get ignored. I'm not sure why, because it's a fantastic walk.

If you want to see Bologna from above, and are not up for climbing the 498 steps of the Torre Degli Asinelli, take the scenic route to San Michele in Bosco. The walk is only about 30 minutes from Piazza Maggiore, and once you reach the courtyard of the church, you will find a fantastic view of Bologna's skyline, a view that you will not see going up to San Luca.

Start from Piazza Maggiore, take Via D'Azeglio until it ends at the outer circle where it meets Porta San Mamolo. Note though that Porta San Mamolo is no longer standing. The city demolished it in the early 1900, when a new urban plan implemented, which included removing much of its surrounding medieval walls. Thankfully, many of the other porte are still standing. However, there are only very small sections of the old walls left.

There are a number of interesting pauses as you walk along Via D'Azeglio. At the corner of Via D'Azeglio and Piazza de Celestini, turn and look at the wall facing opposite the entrance of the church, you will see a large silhouette of a man playing a saxophone. This is a commemoration of Lucio Dalla, a very famous Italian musician, born in Bologna and who died in 2012. The silhouette is on the external wall of his apartment. During most evenings around 6:00pm, one of Lucio's songs is played on speakers set-up on the street-side of the apartment.

Once you cross Via Farini, and continue along Via D'Azeglio, you will pass a number of grand historic Palazzi. One is Palazzo Bevillacqua at Via D'Azeglio 31. The palazzo was built in the late 1400s, and its style is considered un-Bolognese, with its large grey stone façade, and absence of portici. Sometimes, private visits can be organized directly with the palazzo's administrator. Another is the Ex Ospedale dei Bastardini at Via D'Azeglio 41, and across the street, the Ex Ospedale Maternità[34] in Via D'Azeglio 56. The Ex Ospedale Maternità began as a refuge for people in need, like young unwed mothers-to-be. It kept this purpose from the 1300's to 1860, until it was converted into a full-fledged hospital. Now it is privately owned, and can sometimes be visited when its doors are open for special events. The Ex Ospedale dei Bastardini is a palazzo from the 1200s. In 1797, as its name suggests, it became a place that cared for the orphans left by the unwed mothers. This palazzo has also become a great venue for events.

At Porta San Mamolo, cross the street and walk along Via San Mamolo, staying on the left-hand sidewalk. The second street on your left is Via Alessandro Codovilla. Turn and start to walk along this street, keeping to the right-hand sidewalk. After some meters, you will see a small park, with greenery and benches, and a small gate marking the entrance to the park. Push the gate open, enter into the park, and walk along the path parallel to Via Codovilla. You will reach the beginning of a hill, where you'll find a winding path that climbs up the hill. Follow this path, until you reach San Michele in Bosco. During the summer, this walk is a great way to escape the heat of the city, and grab some fresh air offered by the surrounding trees and vegetation.

As you climb up the hill, you will see some of the old villas and palazzi of the Bolognese aristocracy, sitting among the greenery of the surrounding hills or 'Colli Bolognesi'. When you reach San Michele, you will find a different view – the skyline of Bologna. Below is a foto showing the view. There is also a plaque in front of the hedges, which describes some of the key monuments you are looking at.

The actual church[35] has been restored many times since the medieval era, and its façade is more typical of the renaissance period. It also served many different purposes, like a military barracks, a prison during the Napoleon times, and also a residence for the King of Italy. The adjacent monastery is now the Istituto Ortopedico Rizzoli[36] (Rizzoli Orthopaedic Institute), a renowned orthopaedic research hospital. There is actually an entrance directly to the institute via a door inside the church.

To return to Bologna's centre, you can either retrace the route that you took to arrive, or you can walk down the road that passes along the right of the church, called Salita di San Benedetto (on the right side when facing the Bologna skyline). At the end, turn left onto Via Vittorio Putti, and follow it until you reach Via Castiglione. You will pass many large villas, giving you a sense of a different lifestyle in the colli Bolognesi, compared to life in the historic centre.

Turn left onto Via Castiglione, and continue walking until you reach the entrance to the Giardini Margherita, a large park that the Bolognesi use for relaxation, sport, or refuge from the summer heat. You can either explore the Giardini or simply continue down Via Castiglione.

By about this time in the walk, you are likely getting thirsty. You will see the entrance to the <u>Serre dei Giardini Margherita</u>[37] on via Castiglione. 'Serre' is the Italian word for greenhouse. This space was an old greenhouse that has been refurbished into a venue for aperitivo, light food and more. It's a great spot to relax during the day, and to meet friends in the evening.

You can return back to the centre from Porta Castiglione, or even from Porta Santo Stefano if you chose to walk through the Giardini. Once you've passed through either Porta, both streets, Via Castiglione and Via Santo Stefano, will take you right to Bologna's two Towers. They also offer picturesque views of the Bolognese architecture, with unique churches to explore, portici to follow, and towers to admire. If you need to satisfy a gelato craving, make a pit-stop at <u>La Sobetteria Castiglione</u> in Via Castiglione or the <u>Cremeria Santo Stefano</u>[38] in Via Santo Stefano. Both are popular for their great quality gelato.

Mmmm gelato, I'm already getting a craving.

Heading out to search for these hidden spots makes visiting and living in Bologna a gratifying experience. It's difficult to be bored when you can always find something new to explore. It's also very gratifying for us when we listen to the enthusiastic stories of our guests the next day.

4.3
Circumventing the rules – a common Italian pastime

When touring Bologna with a local, they will likely share the story of the secret of one of Bologna's most well known landmarks, la Fontana del Nettuno, or Neptune's Fountain.

You will meet Neptune as you enter Piazza Nettuno, a smaller square that leads to Bologna's large central square, Piazza Maggiore. Neptune is the bronze centrepiece of the fountain, and is surrounded by four topless sirens, who sit there with water jetting out from their nipples.

The statue itself depicts Neptune as a muscular, nude and imposing god, more than 3 meters tall. The fact that he's nude is interesting, as the fountain was ordered by Pope Pio IV in 1563. Travelling around Italy, you will notice many examples where statues, which were originally nude, were covered up with the traditional fig leaf or other concealing item, to appease the conservative catholic authorities. Neptune however, continues to stand proudly nude.

When a Bolognese first introduces you to Neptune, he or she will launch into a short story explaining that when the sculptor designed the statue, the church authority intervened, directing him to endow Neptune with a small, modest penis. The sculptor, a Flemish artist named Jean de Boulogne, seemed to have followed this order.

However, when entering Piazza Nettuno, the Bolognese will guide you to a spot a number of meters behind and to the right of Neptune. Look closely at the statue from this angle, focusing on the hip area, and you will see what looks like a large erect penis protruding from the front. This illusion is broken when you walk around the statue, and see that what looked like an erect penis is actually the thumb and fingers that the sculptor positioned on the outstretched arm and hand of Neptune.

This story is a perfect analogy of Italian's relationship with rules and laws. Like many aspects of the Italian culture, Italians react to rules in a contradictory way. Some rules are steadfastly followed, and others seem created to be circumvented.

Let's look at coffee for example. Italians will not drink coffee with milk after 12:00. It's just not done. Only a tourist will order a cappuccino or caffè macchiato in the afternoon. If you like to receive looks of pity, try to order a cappuccino after dinner.

I'm not a coffee drinker, and prefer hot chocolate instead. It didn't take me long to learn to never order a hot chocolate in the summer in Italy. Last time I ordered a hot chocolate in June, the waiter was incredulous, responding that hot chocolate is only for the winter time, because it is hot. I replied that coffee is also a hot drink and they serve coffee all year round, but had no luck. The waiter just replied that it isn't available, even though it's made simply by adding a packet of pre-mixed chocolate powder to milk, and heating it.

On the other hand, other rules and laws seem to be treated more like suggestions, and people will do whatever possible to go around them. Be forewarned though - think very carefully before deciding not to follow a rule. There are many different systems to monitor adherence to laws, and if there is a control, the penalties are costly. Operating outside the rules can also make you vulnerable to private citizens who have time on their hands to launch a lawsuit, or 'causa', especially if they are riding their moral high-horse, or are brimming with jealousy.

Before jumping into opening a Bed and Breakfast in Italy, it is absolutely critical that you inform yourself of all the different legal obligations. There are numerous laws governing the start-up and operations of a Bed and Breakfast, which are defined by different levels of government.

First and foremost, in Italy the ability to operate a Bed and Breakfast is set out in law at the regional level, not at the country / state level. There is a country wide law that recognizes the importance of tourism and speaks to removing barriers for tourism operators, especially small and medium sized business. However, it delegates powers to the regions. (Legge 29 marzo 2001, n. 135, "Riforma della legislazione nazionale del turismo"[39]) This means that each region has the authority to decide if it will permit B&Bs to operate in their region, and within which boundaries or restrictions. For example, in some regions, Bed and Breakfasts are prevented from serving food for breakfast that is cooked on premises. Rather they can only serve items pre-packaged or prepared by authorized food service establishments.

Emilia-Romagna has different regulations for the many different types of accommodation. Luckily, everything can be found on the region's website http://imprese.regione.emilia-romagna.it/turismo[40]. If you are considering opening a Bed and Breakfast in Emilia-Romagna, you should learn the laws for the following two types of accommodation: the '**Bed and Breakfast**', and the '**Affittacamere–Room and Breakfast–Locanda**'. The region actually created a helpful summary[41] of the differences between these two main categories to minimize confusion.

If you choose to operate under the Bed and Breakfast category, there are some key restrictions to be aware of. First, you can only offer a maximum of 3 rooms, with up to 2 people per room. You also need to have your residence registered in the B&B, i.e. you need to officially live there. More importantly, you cannot be open all year round. Instead, you can be open for either 120 days in a year, or for 500 'pernottamenti' (calculated by the number of people hosted per night, not by the number of rooms booked per night). Additionally, you cannot publicize your B&B on websites where the public can make direct bookings. Instead, you can be present on sites where only your contact information is featured.

The benefit of operating as a B&B is that you do not need to register as a business. You run it as a private citizen. Your earnings will be taxed as personal income, and not as a business, which is much less complicated and at lower tax rates.

On the other hand, a Room and Breakfast is considered a business. You obtain your business number, register it at the local chamber of commerce, and manage your accounting as you would any other business. While you will likely pay higher taxes, you can offer up to 6 rooms, and there are no limitations on the number of days you can be open, or where you publicize your property.

One of the most important pieces of advice I can offer is to find yourself a capable 'Commercialista'. Do not try to understand the income and tax implications on your own. The personal and commercial tax system in Italy is extremely complex, and laws change annually. A Commercialista, is a profession similar to a tax accountant in North America. He or she can explain the implications, model your potential income, and help you choose the best option.

When we first opened our Bed and Breakfast, we didn't know what our occupancy would be, and whether we would reach the 120 day or 500 pernottamenti limit. So we decided to start with registering it a 'Bed and Breakfast'. Once we saw the rate of reservations coming in, we decided to change and register it as a Room and Breakfast, so that we would not be restricted and forced to close once we reached the limit.

Now, you may be thinking, it's Italy - does everyone really follow the rules? A quick scan on the internet will show you a very large number of Bed and Breakfasts, and even apartments or rooms for rent in Emilia Romagna, which are open all year round and listed on reservation sites where you can make direct bookings. Are they are all operating as a Room and Breakfast as they should be, or are they registered as a Bed and Breakfast, and circumventing the laws? Or are they even registered?

If they are circumventing the laws, it's at their own risk. Should there be a control, the electronic paper trail is readily available. For example, the booking systems can be an easy source to confirm the number of bookings and revenue generated throughout the year. A few months ago, we received a visit from one of the sales representatives from a major international booking site, who mentioned that there had been some controls recently, and some B&Bs need to shut down as they could not afford the fines.

For us, the risk isn't worth it. Our Bed and Breakfast is an important part of our income, and we don't want to leave it to chance. Being in a condominium, we also prefer to avoid offering potentially disgruntled neighbours the opportunity to shut us down, in case they decide that they dislike having a B&B in their building.

So we try our best to be law abiding good citizens :-).

4.4
Don't forget the red tape...

We decided to visit the Bologna Welcome tourist information office, located in Piazza Maggiore, to ask for copies of Bologna's tourist city map to give to our guests when they arrive. All visitors, when arriving to a new town, want to know how to get around, what to see and do, and where to eat. Our guests **really** appreciate it when we provide them with a map and explain where to go.

We walked in the office, and approached one of the employees, standing behind the main counter.

'Hi. We run a Bed and Breakfast in Bologna, and would like to ask you for copies of the tourist city map to give to guests when they arrive.'

'We can only give you 2 or 3 maps. We do not hand out large quantities,' the employee responded.

'We have 3 rooms and are registered with the city. We usually hand out 3 maps a day. Is there anything you can do? I asked.

'You can direct your guests to come to this office for a copy,' she offered.

'But they need a map when they arrive, so that we can show them how to get to the piazza,' I tried to explain. 'Why would it matter to Bologna Welcome if the visitor gets a copy of the map at their hotel, instead of this office, as long as they have the map?'

'We don't have enough printed maps to hand out to all the hotels,' she explained.

That's logical, I thought sarcastically - print out only a limited number of maps so that only a portion of visitors can get a copy.

This conversation was going nowhere. Maybe a different approach was needed.

'Perhaps we can request a specific quantity of maps directly from the city's tourism department?' I asked hopefully.

'Sorry, it isn't possible. The city's tourism department does not order the maps. The map, however, is available on our website in different languages. I suggest you print your own copies for your guests.'

Brilliant, like we didn't already think of that.

'Yes, that's an option,' I replied. 'And that is what we are currently doing. Except, printing out the maps is at our cost, and printer ink isn't cheap. As an accommodation establishment in Bologna, we collect the city's tourism tax from each guest, and send the money to the city. It would be reasonable to think that in return, the city could arrange to make maps easily available.'

'Sorry. You can either keep returning to this office and we can provide you with a small number of maps each time, or your guests can come here to request the map, or you can print them yourself for your guests'.

That was a waste of time. We thanked her for the few maps she gave us, and left the tourism office.

Like almost all cities in Italy, and even across Europe, tourists are asked to pay a nightly city tax. In Bologna, the amount of the tax depends on the actual price of the room, and can range from 1.50€ to 5.00€, per person, per night (up to a maximum of 5 nights). While it isn't as expensive as cities like Rome, it isn't pocket change either.

I have nothing against the tax. However, a portion of it could be reinvested to make the tourist experience the best possible. Great word-of-mouth reviews from tourists will lead to more visitors, and will contribute to more tax revenues.

Bologna has already invested in the contract with Bologna Welcome, which is actually a private vendor responsible for promoting the city and welcoming visitors. The tourism office and website were recently redone, and look professional. The office is also in a prime space, right in Piazza Maggiore.

However, not all tourists end up visiting the office. The first welcome to Bologna actually takes place when a tourist arrives at their hotel. We spend at least 10 minutes with each guest during their check-in, walking them through the map of Bologna, and describing the main sites, neighbourhoods and restaurants to visit.

This type of short-sightedness can be frustrating. It's also irritating considering the administration work we are required to do on a daily basis for the various government offices involved with tourism.

If you are planning to open a B&B, spend the time to educate yourself on the rules and red-tape, before you actually open. Don't expect to be handed all the information in a neat package. In Italy, you will need to become accustomed to the idea that it's your responsibility to get informed, while no one takes responsibility for doing the informing.

> **B&B Owner Tip:** In Italy, you will need to register your B&B with the city. Call the departments responsible for tourism, to ask them about rules and requirements. Before actually visiting the offices, ask them about the forms you need to complete, and the documents you need to bring with you. This will help you save a lot of time. Don't expect different departments to communicate or share information with each other. You will likely be visiting multiple offices.
>
> If the forms indicate that copies are needed, the employees will likely not the make photocopies for you. They will just turn you away. Make the copies beforehand, and bring them with you.
>
> One final thought - call ahead to ask about office opening hours. Different department offices have different opening hours. They will not all be open 9am to 5pm, Monday to Friday.

Although I was expecting to be drowned in red-tape to start the B&B, the process was actually painless, and only took a couple of days to complete.

One of the requirements to run a B&B in Bologna is to register at the city's Dipartimento Economia e Promozione della Città. There is a form to fill out and documents, like your blueprints, to attach. Once ready, I brought my documents to the department's office, where they stamped a copy for my records.

Next, you will need to visit the city's Ufficio Riscossione e Controlli, as they are responsible for the Imposta di Soggiorno, or tourism tax. There, I provided the details of the B&B again, and they created a profile and gave me the login details to the city's website, where we need to make the declarations and payments for the tourism tax.

Emilia Romagna's regional office of Servizio Turismo e Commercio also requires a couple of registrations. One is to declare your maximum annual room rates, and the other is to request access to their tourism data collection website, where you are supposed to register the number and origin of all the guests, on a quarterly basis. Luckily, registering for these can be done via fax.

Lastly, you need to visit the Questura di Bologna, the police headquarters. There is another form to complete, and you must show a copy of the stamped registration with the city, to gain access to the police's tourist registration website. In Italy, all accommodation establishments are required to register the details of each guest with the police, after check-in.

So, with all the registrations out of the way, you can now concentrate on running your B&B. Well, almost. As mentioned above, at each check-in, you are required to get the details of the guest's passport or other official ID, and log into the Questura's website to submit the information to the Police. At least it's an easy web-based process.

In preparation for checkout, you are required to log into the city's Imposta di Soggiorno website, enter the details of the guest's stay, and print out the tourism tax receipt for each room. We collect the tax payments from each guest, and every three months, we make a bank transfer to the city, for all the tax money we collected.

Don't forget that there are also the tourism statistics on number and origin of the guests to submit quarterly to the Region's database.

All this effort, for the opportunity to run a B&B... and we are then told that we also need to print out the city's tourism map at our cost.

4.5
The two Sicilians

This story is more light-hearted, which we enjoy sharing with our friends. It's about two guests, let's call them Marco and Gino, in their 50s, from the island of Sicily. They came to Bologna for one of the major international trade fairs hosted in the city.

Like many cities, when a fair is in town, the hotel situation becomes impossible. Room prices skyrocket, and all the rooms in the city are usually booked a year in advanced. These two gentlemen were colleagues, and were sharing a room for a few days, while they attended the fair.

B&B Owner Tip: Double Bed versus 2 Twin Beds? Why not offer both options! When considering what type of beds to arrange in the rooms, we decided to place two single beds in each room. Each single bed has a sturdy base, and a comfortable tall mattress. When we have couples who prefer a queen bed, we attach the bases, and place an additional queen mattress (a few centimetres in thickness) on top of the single beds so that the guests do not feel the separate mattresses.

If there are guests who prefer two separate single beds, we remove the top queen mattress and separate the beds to easily accommodate the guests' request. This gives us a lot of flexibility to meet the different needs of guests, and we would recommend it for any B&B.

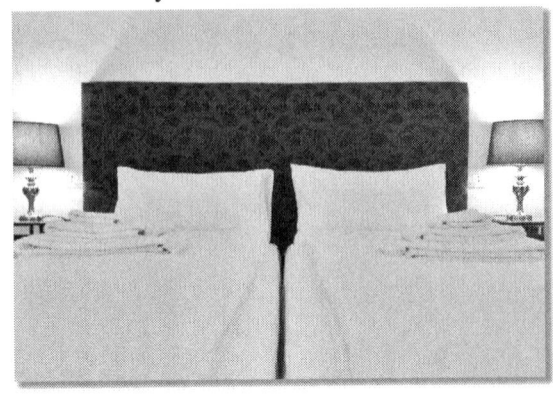

A couple of days before the arrival of Marco and Gino, we sent out our customary introduction email, asking them to confirm their arrival time. We do this for every guest, and while it's time consuming, it helps us organize our free time and social life around the different arrival times. The reply we received advised us that they will be arriving by flight, and should be at our B&B at around 7:00pm. On the evening of their arrival, 7:00pm came and passed, but Marco and Gino hadn't arrived. 8:00pm passed, and there was still no sign of them.

I called the telephone number on their reservation, and the person that answered mentioned that she was the agent who made the reservation for Marco and Gino. I explained that they hadn't arrived, and she replied that she would try to call them. She called back a couple of minutes later.

'They told me that their plane is delayed and that they should arrive at your B&B in about an hour', she said. I asked her for their flight number, which she didn't have with her. I said that I would search for their revised time of arrival by the departure city, on the website of Bologna's airport.

After hanging up, I visited the airport's website. Something was strange...the flight had landed on time. I re-dialled the agent and informed her that the flight had arrived on time. She replied that she didn't know what was happening, and gave me the personal number of one of the guests, so that I could call him directly to ask when they would be arriving.

Ok, time to make another call. I dialled the number, and Marco responded. In the background, I could hear music blasting and many people conversing loudly. It sounded like a party. I calmly explained to Marco that we were waiting for them, and asked him when they would arrive. He started explaining that a friend had met them at the airport, and that they were at a restaurant now. 'We will be there around midnight', Marco advised. I asked Marco to call me directly on my cell if there was going to be another change. José and I then went out to have aperitivo with some friends.

We returned home before midnight to wait for Marco and Gino. 1:00am passed, and they still didn't arrive. Grabbing the phone, I called Marco again. He said that they are on their way. Around 1:30am, Marco called, saying that they were near, but couldn't find the street address. After guiding them with directions via telephone, they finally arrived.

At last we could go to sleep!

Breakfast the next morning was the normal routine. We chatted with all the guests, including Marco and Gino, and they left to make their way to the trade fair. José then started the daily housekeeping of the rooms.

As José began cleaning Marco and Gino's room, he noticed something odd. There was only one towel hanging in the bathroom.

For each guest, we provide a facecloth, as well as a medium and large bath towel. We also leave a bath mat in the bathroom. This means that in Marco and Gino's room, there should be a total of six towels, plus one bath mat. Instead, he could only find one towel. Scanning the room, he noticed one of their suitcases partially opened, and could actually see the white of our towels from the opening.

Did they place our towels in their luggage to keep them out of the way in their room? Or were they planning to take the towels home with them?

They were staying a couple more nights, and we decided to not yet say anything.

That day and night passed, uneventful. The next day, while cleaning, José noticed that the towels were still missing. At this point, we were really interested to see what would happen.

The morning after was their check-out. During breakfast, Marco and Gino were chatty, asking questions like did we own land in Bologna, how much did the apartment cost, and so on. José continued to converse with them until they finished eating and were ready to check-out. They settled their bill, returned to their room to gather their luggage, and then prepared to depart. They said goodbye to José and left the B&B.

As soon as our door closed, José went to check their room. Sure enough, all the towels were gone, even the bath mat.

José left the apartment quickly to catch up with Marco and Gino. He could hear them in the stairwell, as they had decided not to take the elevator.

'Where are our towels?' José asked as he reached Marco and Gino.

'Towels?' Marco responded somewhat flustered.

'Yes, all the towels that we provided in the room are missing,' José replied.

'But - but we thought the towels were ours. Our wives had packed them for us.' Marco tried to explain.

'No, they are the towels of the Bed and Breakfast,' José repeated.

At this point Marco already started to open the suitcases. 'But these aren't our towels to take? Gino said that they are for the guests and we can take them', Marco explained.

'No. They are not your towels to take. They belong to the Bed and Breakfast.' José replied. José was finding the conversation comical, and was replying calmly and firmly.

Marco and Gino handed the towels to José, while Marco continued to mutter that they had thought the towels were theirs.

José thanked them and returned to the apartment. He couldn't stop laughing. He compared the comical conversation to something out of an old Pasolini or Felini film.

Looking out the window, the scene continued, as he watched them crossing the street, Gino walking ahead, with Marco in tow. Marco was still talking and gesturing animatedly. Gino just continued to walk, shaking his head and not saying a word.

4.6
The case of the exploding shower-heads

One morning, a guest came out of their room to let us know that their shower-head exploded. They had turned the water on, heard a loud bang, looked up and saw a crack right through the diameter of the shower-head. We examined the shower-heads in the other bathrooms, and realized that 3 out of the 4 shower-heads were cracked.

At least the culprit wasn't elusive.

It was the result of the significant amount of 'calcare', or calcium deposit, in Bologna's water. Calcium had blocked the little nozzles of the shower-head where the water shoots out. When the guest turned the water on, there was a build up of hot water in the shower-head, and it cracked from the pressure.

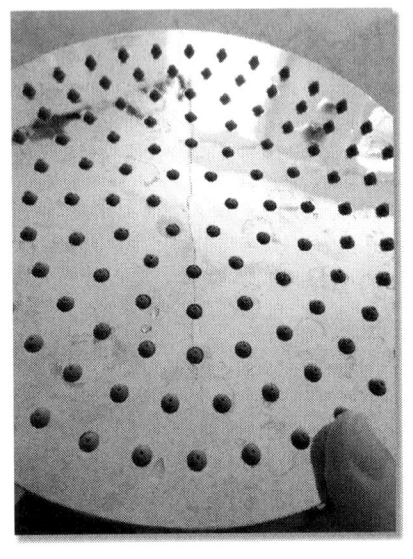

I don't remember ever having to worry about the consequences of heavy calcium deposits in the water back in Canada. In Italy though, it's impossible to ignore. Just wash a glass by hand and leave it to dry, and within a couple of minutes you will see that it's full of spots from the calcium. Also, forget about scrubbing away the calcium from a water boiler or a rice steamer. After just a couple of uses, it will become coated with a thick layer of calcium that is difficult to crack! Even cleaning becomes a difficult chore. We spend a lot of extra time scrubbing away calcium from the shower doors, sinks, and more, and also need to wipe down the cutlery and glasses every day. Vinegar will become your best friend, to help remove calcium deposits.

Guests will ask if the tap water in Bologna is safe to drink. Of course it is. However, I keep thinking about all the calcium that gets left behind. How does the body manage to filter it out? So, I mostly drink bottled water. Each day we also leave a couple of complimentary bottles of water for guests in their mini-bar.

We try to extend the life of our small appliances like the electric water boilers and coffee makers, by only using bottled water. However, we can't use bottled water for the larger appliances. Instead, there is a wide selection of anti-calcare products to apply with appliances like the dishwasher and washing machine. Never forget to add the anti-calcare to every load of laundry you do.

Unfortunately, we still keep learning that we need to pay closer attention to all the plumbing fixtures, just like the shower-heads. This means closer inspections for calcium deposits, and regular rinses with anti-calcium cleaning liquids.

This also applies to the toilets. We had numerous instances where once a toilet was flushed, the water would not stop flowing from the water tank. There were even a couple of times where a guest left their room, not realizing that the toilet continued flushing, and returned hours later to see the toilet still flushing. Imagine our anger after realizing how much water was wasted from a toilet continuously flushing for hours.

After calls and visits from the construction company who installed the toilets, as well as a visit from the actual supplier of the toilets, we learned that the calcium left by the water in the toilet's water tank, prevented the levers and valves from working properly. Once a month now, we add anti-calcare liquid to the water tanks of all the toilets.

It's a constant struggle, and the only solutions are a preventative maintenance schedule, effective anti-calcare products, and good old fashion elbow-grease.

So get on your knees and scrub, scrub, scrub!

4.7
The tortellini experience

What type of adopted Bolognese can I call myself if I can't cook the traditional cuisine? The region is the home of pasta, so that seems like the right place to start. The question is - how to learn?

There are a variety of cooking schools in Bologna, which can satisfy the ambitions and schedules of almost everyone. However, running the B&B makes it is almost impossible to commit to any course that has a set schedule. The check-in times of our guests depend on things like flight times, train schedules, driving arrangements and more, and we adapt our availability around the daily arrival times. Guests usually confirm their expected arrival time only a few days before their arrival. This makes managing our private calendar a continuous challenge.

If I'm going to learn to cook Bolognese, I prefer to learn from a person born and raised in Bologna, who cooks the typical dishes for their family at home. I would also like to learn in a more casual, personal setting, with fewer people.

So every time our friend Carlo mentions that he and his partner Giovanni, are heading to his parent's for a meal prepared by his mother, I tease him by asking, 'When will your mother invite us for lunch and teach us how to cook Bolognese?' Carlo is one of the few true Bolognese that we know, born and raised in the neighbourhood Bolognina, just outside the city centre.

I met Carlo and Giovanni at the habitual Sunday evening aperitivo held in the same bar where I met Domenico, our friend and architect. Correction, I re-met Carlo and Giovanni at that bar.

I actually first met Carlo and Giovanni about a year before moving to Bologna. My ex and I had planned a weekend trip to Bologna for the city's annual Pride parade. The parade was energizing, and the streets were full of people socializing. That night, we went to the main party being held at a clubbing venue in Parco Nord, outside the city centre. We were outside the main dance area grabbing some air, when we started chatting with Carlo and Giovanni. Both of them were very friendly, and easy to talk with. They introduced us to their friends, and we passed much of our evening with them chatting and dancing.

Giovanni was also my first instructor in how to handle the Italian queue, or line-up. If you've ever been at the boarding lounge of an Italian airport, or waited for a bus at the bus stop, you will notice that Italians do not form a line. The first-come first-served concept is somewhat foreign in Italy – it's not in their DNA. Instead, you find a mass of people huddling and pushing, trying to get ahead of one-another.

Giovanni and I had gone to the bar to order drinks, and there, we found a mass of about 25-30 people crowding around a small bar, with only a couple of bartenders serving drinks.

'This is impossible' I told Giovanni. 'We'll be here all night waiting our turn to get a drink.'

Giovanni looked at me 'You need to get through the crowd until you reach the bar.'

'Ok, but how?'

'Find open spaces, position your body at an angle, and press through where there's the least resistance,' he explained.

Sure enough, within a couple of minutes, we wedged our way through the crowd, and ended up right at the bar.

On one hand, you feel guilty being served before the many other people who arrived ahead of you. On the other hand, if you wait until everyone before you gets served, you will never be served, as you will need to deal with everyone else jumping ahead of you.

Generally though, if I see something that resembles a line formation, I will respect it and get in line. If someone tries to sneak ahead of me, I will speak up and tell them to get to the back of the line. The typical response is 'Oh, there's a line? I didn't notice it.' I never realized how a line of people can be invisible to the naked eye.

The pride party continued and we had a fantastic evening. We even exchanged numbers to stay in touch. Although, we never did contact them again, as my ex and I became consumed with our difficulties back home in Milano.

A few months after moving to Bologna, I went to the Sunday aperitivo, and saw Carlo and Giovanni at the bar ordering drinks. Over a year and a half passed since we first met. I recognizing them, and walked up and said hi.

Since then, we have passed many evenings together over aperitivo, dinner or exploring the latest exhibition or show.

With summer vacations over, and everyone starting to get back into the working rhythm of early September, I asked Carlo again when his mother would teach us some Bolognese cooking. This time, his said 'Ok, let's organize. I will speak with my mother, and we can arrange a lesson during one of the next couple of weekends.'

We agreed on a Sunday, and I offered to host the lesson with Carlo's mother, Paola, at our home. This way, we could manage the check-in of the guests, no matter what time they arrived.

The menu was set. For our first lesson, we would make Tortellini in Brodo. This is the quintessential Bolognese dish, and is on the menu of any good trattoria. The small tortellini are usually filled with a combination of pork, mortadella, prosciutto and parmigiano. The tradition in Bologna is to eat them in a broth, not a sauce. The broth is made from a base of different cuts of beef and part of a hen. It's absolutely delicious, especially in the fall and winter months.

It's not the easiest meal to start with though, because once you've learned to make the pasta dough, you then have to cut, fill and shape each individual tortellino. I like a challenge.

Paola sent us the list of ingredients, and instructions on how to make the broth, as the broth would need to be made the evening before.

There is a macelleria (butcher shop) around the corner from us, which I am embarrassed to say, I had not yet visited. This was the perfect excuse to make our first visit, and what a great surprise. The store is called La Macelleria, and is located in Via G. Ercolani 1. The owners are a husband and wife, Luciana and Fabio, and their son

Matteo. We entered and explained that our friend's mother was going to teach us how to prepare tortellini in brodo, and handed them Paola's list of ingredients.

They had all the right cuts of meat, and even suggested alternative cuts depending on the quality that we were looking for. They also had prosciutto and mortadella, as well as the parmigiano reggiano aged 30 months, which the recipe asks for. As they were preparing the meats, they explained that each family has their own variation of the recipe, with some recipes calling for different mixes of meats for the broth, or even different ratios of the ingredients for the tortellini filling.

They asked us if we wanted 'gli odori', which they would offer for free. 'Gli odori' literally means 'the odours', and I didn't understand what they were referring to. Not wanting to look stupid, I said 'sure'. Luciana grabbed a bag and went to get the carrot, celery and onion needed for the broth. When I returned home, I sent a quick message to Carlo and his mother to let them know that we had all the ingredients, and asked if the vegetables for the stock are called 'gli odori'. They confirmed that Bolognesi use the expression 'gli odori', likely 'perchè profumano il brodo' - because they add scent to the broth.

I prepared the broth the Saturday before the lesson, following the recipe closely. I was surprised at how much fat melted from the meat. When I poured the broth into a couple of containers to place in the fridge, there was a layer of fat at the top almost half a centimetre thick. Thankfully, we will be removing the fat before heating the broth, to protect our poor arteries.

Giovanni and Paola were the first to arrive, bringing all the necessary equipment. They supplied the really large tagliere (wooden cutting board) needed to make the pasta dough, the manual meat grinder for the tortellini filling, the pasta press and pasta drying rack, and more. We will need to go equipment shopping if we want to make tortellini again ourselves.

Paola even showed us the original recipe for the tortellini filling, which her mother had written down decades before. She explained that the word 'Dose' at the top (also 'dose in English), was the old Bolognese term for 'ricetta', or recipe. Also, the word 'forma' beneath 'mortadella' was the popular reference to 'parmigiano reggiano' or parmesan cheese. Note also the Mussolini-esc image of the eagle or 'aquila' at the bottom of the notepad, from the industrial rubber producer where Paola's father had worked.

Paola was a fantastic teacher. She was patient, quick-witted and had a great sense of humour. In the kitchen, with her apron on and handkerchief covering her hair, her looks are somewhat deceiving. You would never think that this elderly Italian mother graduated university in physics, and spent her life teaching mathematics in high school.

I ended up taking many fotos and video throughout the afternoon to document the entire process. I've even compiled the afternoon into an illustrative recipe that is included at the end of this book, in case you would like to try making your own Tortellini in Brodo.

The process is labour intensive, and seems to have been designed to be done in the company of family and friends. Each tortellino takes time to shape. It's also a bit of a race to shape the tortellini before the sheet of pasta becomes too cool and dry to manipulate. The process requires patience, especially if you are just starting to learn. If we placed too much filling, or weren't gentle enough, the tortellino would break. No one was upset though, because each time someone broke a tortellino, they would simply pop it in their mouth and eat it. Nobody seemed concerned that it was uncooked pasta dough.

In the end, we had a spread of fantastic tortellini, not necessarily all in the right shape or size. It didn't matter - it was our first time, even for Carlo, and the tortellini would have the same great taste going down.

We brought the broth back to a boil, cooked the tortellini, and savoured our hard work with some delicious red wine.

After all the effort, we now have a new appreciation for the energy and time that goes into making hand-made tortellini. José mentioned that next time, he will not comment on the price of tortellini at the market, knowing now what it takes to make a couple of servings.

We also discussed our potential next lesson over dinner. I think we agreed on Tagliatelle al Ragù`. I've talked enough about this favourite hearty pasta dish in my stories. It's about time to learn how to make the original dish. I can't wait!

4.8
You can't satisfy everyone

We recently received our lowest review rating ever. The review arrived at the start of our winter trip to Sicily. If you haven't yet discovered the stunning Sicilian towns and ancient archaeological sites, make it one of your next trips!

My cell buzzed with a notification message from one of the reservation sites where we are listed. I quickly looked at the message, and saw that a new guest review had been posted. Opening the message, I was honestly shocked to see the review rating at almost one-half of our average rating. The actual comments weren't written in English, but with the languages that José and I know, we were able to understand what was written. The reviewer and home country were also identified, and we remembered the middle-aged couple who stayed with us for a few nights about a month before.

Reading the comments, I felt incredulous and hurt, all wrapped-up in a bundle of just f'n pissed. I vented for the next couple of minutes. Most of the comments weren't warranted, and some were just false. The review was aimed to hurt. I guess it's easy to write what you want, when you can hide behind the impersonal screen of a computer.

We take immense pride in providing all our guests the best possible experience, and by the end of 2015, we were in the top 2 best-rated B&Bs in Bologna, out of almost 100 B&Bs on the reservation site. We try to create a relationship with all of our guests, and to go that extra mile by sharing suggestions on where to go and what to see, providing advice and reservations for taxis and restaurants, and more. They see that we love our work, and that we rely on their support to continue to spread the word. This is our livelihood.

The experience with this couple was off from the start. We contact all of our guests a couple of days before their arrival to confirm their arrival time. With these guests, we sent our customary introduction email, and then sent an SMS and also tried to call their telephone number, but never received a response.

On their arrival day, we waited and wondered if they would show-up. Eventually they did, and were already upset. First, they said that they didn't realize they booked a Bed and Breakfast, and were expecting a hotel. Then they had trouble finding our address and entry door. Unfortunately, we didn't yet have a sign outside the main door, as the approval was stuck in administrative limbo, but that is another story. We anticipate this by including instructions in our welcome message, which they said they did not see.

We explained our challenges with the sign, and gave the guests a warm welcome. We then went through our check-in routine. There was a bit of a language barrier, but it seemed like it went smoothly.

The next morning, the husband arrived first for breakfast. We asked him if they slept well, and he responded that his wife had trouble sleeping. Asking why, he explained that she didn't feel safe, because when they returned from dinner the night before, they had found the main entrance door of the building open.

We reassured him that they should feel secure. Our B&B is also our home, where we live, and Bologna is a safe city. We explained that there are a number of different security measures, including video cameras at the main entrance and hallway of the building. There is also the entrance door of our B&B, which is a 'porta blindata', a very thick, almost armoured door. Guests can only open the door by entering a code on the keypad, which we change every week. Furthermore, guests keep their rooms locked with their room keys. This makes more locked doors to pass through than most hotels.

Strange, it was the first time we received this comment. Then I remembered the vacation I had taken to our guests' home country, a number of years before. During the trip, hotel staff indicated neighbourhoods to avoid, and some locals described problems with theft and gangs in the bigger cities. There were also neighbourhoods where people lived in gated complexes. I thought that maybe they believed there were similar issues in Bologna. I mentioned to the guest that Bologna doesn't have the same problems as those in his country. Oops - that was a mistake. He quickly replied that there were no issues with safety in his country.

I then tried to explain that many guests actually tell us that the door to our B&B is like Fort Knox, but he didn't seem interested in our reassurances.

The breakfasts and interactions over the next couple of days seemed to go much better. The wife described that she was sleeping well, and we thought that maybe we succeeded in making them feel comfortable and satisfied.

The morning of checkout, they had wanted to reserve a taxi to go to the central train station, and then from the station take the local bus to the airport. José recommended that instead, they should take a taxi directly to the airport, explaining that they would actually save money. They were grateful for the suggestion, and José made the call to reserve the taxi.

When it came time to settle the bill though, the husband did not want to pay bologna's city tax. Most cities in Europe now charge a tax of a couple of Euros per tourist, per night. The husband insisted that the tax should be included in the rate, which it wasn't. He pointed to the IVA tax on his reservation confirmation, and José described that IVA is the regular good and services tax charged throughout Europe. José firmly insisted that it was the guest's responsibility to pay the city tax, and after attempting to debate it some more, the husband finally paid it.

Now, about a month later, they left a review. In the review however, instead of describing their issue with paying the city tax, and their sense of security, they included comments like we serve a poor breakfast, and that we watch the guests during breakfast to control how much they consume. They also wrote that we provide only one coffee per guest during breakfast. Are you kidding? For breakfast, we set up a buffet every morning that includes freshly sliced cured meats, a selection of cheeses, breads, croissants, fruit, cereals, and jams, as well as a home-made cake. We also prepare and serve fresh coffee and tea, and provide a selection of juices. Guests can, and do, ask for refills, which we serve. We are there to replenish the breakfast items, and always ask all guests if they would like anything else. Guests can also make themselves coffee and tea during the day, as we also leave complimentary coffee, tea and water for them in their rooms.

How can they be allowed to leave comments that were false? I wrote a message to the reservation site explaining the situation, and the reasons why we disagreed with the review. They replied saying that the review followed their policy, and that we should write a reply to the review. Really? Their policy allows people to write false statements? I responded, requesting to receive the details of their policy. I asked whether their policy permits guests to write false statements, as this puts us in a position to defend ourselves against untrue comments. I never received a response.

Instead of responding immediately to the review, I let it rest a week. I didn't want to write something that might convey our emotions instead of the facts. I let it marinate, until I was happy with how I would articulate responses to all of their points.

I think that if we ever face a similar situation where a client arrives unsatisfied from the start, I will suggest that they call the booking site and make a new reservation elsewhere, without a cancellation penalty from us. A happy B&B is one where people are happy to be there.

4.9
Comedy of errors

Sometimes in Italy, you will be shocked at how smoothly you can get through an administrative process. For example, once we were ready to start the apartment renovations, our architect only needed to submit a series of online forms to the city to communicate the start of the work (the CIL – Comunicazione di inizio lavori). There was no need to wait for a review of the blueprints, or an approval of a permit. The city responded with a registration number, and the demolition could start.

Other times however, you can find yourself stuck in an infinite loop of red tape. You will witness a cascading comedy of errors, which you will pray desperately to end. The only exit is persistence, creativity, and divine patience.

For example, while preparing for the renovations, we also submitted a separate request to another department of the city, asking to reserve two parking spaces on the street just outside the apartment. The plan was to arrange a protected space with a container, so that the workers can dump the debris from our second floor window to the container. It's a very common request, and the approval usually takes 30 days, plus a nice fee of around 5,000 Euros. After a month though, we didn't hear back, and the renovation company started to make calls to find out why. We learned that after we had submitted the request, the city decided to change the designation of the same two spaces from regular parking (indicated by blue lines) to temporary parking for offloading (designated by yellow lines).

Ok, but how does that impact our request? Well, a different office is responsible for managing the parking spaces with the yellow lines. Our request had just been sitting in the original office, and now would need to be sent to the other office for assessment.

The demolition was ready to start though. The construction company had all the workers lined-up, and we couldn't wait another month for the approval. In the end, the construction company decided to manage the removal of the debris the old-fashioned way – by hand. The workers were stuck walking pails full of debris down two stories of stairs, as using the elevators to transport the debris is not permitted.

Another inspiring example of this comedy of errors, is the odyssey to receive approval to place a sign for our B&B outside the building's main entrance.

There was already a sign for another business outside the door of the second entrance to the same building complex, and I hoped that it would be a simple process to place a similar sign for our B&B. I called the condo Administrator to find out what I needed to do, and he explained that I would need to ask approval at the next condo meeting. As a general rule, if you plan to modify the facade of any of public space in the building where you live, you will likely need the approval of the residents.

That's great. Our sign is now dependent on the approval of a majority of the apartment owners. The Administrator asked me to email him the details of the sign, including the proposed dimension, material, and design. He also said that he will include the request for approval on the agenda of the next condo meeting.

'When is the next meeting?' I asked.

'A date hasn't yet been set,' he replied. 'It will likely be in the summer.'

It was February, and the B&B had been open since September.

The delay was irritating, but manageable. We had learned that guests tend to miss the entrance to our building, as the street signs are not easily visible. To compensate, we try to help our guests by contacting them via email before their arrival, and sending them links to maps that show how to reach us by car, or by foot from the train station. However, many guests had suggested that a sign outside the entrance would make their arrival easier.

B&B Owner Tip: Research the various requirements for signage, which can depend on numerous rules and regulations.

For example, you will likely need approval from your condo committee. If the sign is on street level, you may need permission from the city and pay a fee. There may also be requirements for B&B tourism signage, which are set by the region and described in the tourism legislation.

I emailed the proposal to the Administrator, and we waited patiently for the notice of the summer condo meeting to arrive. June came and passed, but we didn't receive the invitation. It was the beginning of July, and I thought that it was unlikely that the meeting would be scheduled for August, because Italy pretty much shuts down during August. Cities become ghost-towns, as everyone leaves en-mass for the beach.

I called the Administrator's office to find out what was happening.

One of the assistants answered, and I explained that I wanted to know the date of the next meeting, as I was waiting to request approval for my sign. 'The meeting was held last week', she replied. 'Excuse me? How could it have already been held? I didn't receive any notice of the meeting.' She explained that they sent the notice via registered mail to everyone. Well then, if they mailed me the notice, why didn't I receive it?

I asked her if my request for the sign was approved in the meeting. She put me on hold to speak with the Administrator, and returned. She explained that there were too many items to discuss in the meeting, and there wasn't enough time to include my request. I would need to wait until the next meeting, which will likely be in the autumn. I explained that I had been waiting since February. She replied that I would need to wait until the next meeting.

She then asked if I had ever sent the office a request to receive all correspondence via email instead of regular mail. I responded that no-one advised me that that was an option, but that I will send her an email with my formal authorization shortly.

I hung up and wrote an email to authorize them to send communications electronically. I also asked them for a copy of the registered mail receipt for the notice of the last meeting, which they supposedly sent to me. I'm still waiting for it.

Shortly afterwards, I did receive via email a copy of the minutes from the meeting held the week before. The meeting started at 18:00, and ended at 20:15. The last sentence of the minutes?

> 'Alle ore 20:15, nulla più essendoci da deliberare, il Presidente, previo lettura del presente verbale, scioglie l'Assemblea'.

The quick translation: 'at 20:15, as there was nothing else to discuss, the meeting was closed.' So I was never sent the announcement of the condo meeting, and the Administrator forgot to include my request on the agenda.

An apology for their errors would have been nice. Canadians sometimes mock themselves at how many times we can say 'sorry' in a day. In Italy however, it's more likely that hell will freeze over before someone admits they made a mistake, and apologizes.

Near the end of September, I finally received an email with the invitation for the next meeting, scheduled in October. I read through the list of agenda items, and what a shock...my request for the sign was not on the agenda. There was a slot for 'other items' at the end of the agenda. I decided that I would print the emails with my proposal that I sent to the Administrator, and at the start of the meeting, request that I be added to the end of the agenda.

I was the first to arrive at the condo meeting, which was held in a local community hall. When the Administrator arrived, I presented myself and reminded him of my request to have the sign approved. He mentioned that he would raise the request at the end.

Let's see, what are my impressions of my first condo meeting in Italy? Where to start... There are at least two assistants in the Administrator's office, yet the Administrator showed up alone. He then requested a volunteer from the participants to take the minutes.

The agenda had nine items, and everyone felt entitled to be able to express their point of view for as long as they wanted, **repeatedly**, during the discussion of **each** item. It was a never-ending dialogue. I felt empathy for the Administrator, who struggled to keep the discussions focused. Yet somehow, he actually managed to successfully steer everyone to reach decisions on each item.

There was also plenty of drama. Some discussions turned personal, and one participant even stormed out. I think I saw the glint of tears in his eyes. Another apartment owner was antagonistic throughout the entire meeting. He seemed to know, and get into everyone's business.

As it was my first meeting, it was also the first time that I was meeting many of the other apartment owners in our building. I had a nagging worry that if someone was opposed to the B&B, they would make it vocal during that meeting.

Sure enough, Mister Antagonistic did find a break in the discussion to raise a question about my B&B. According to him, as I was operating a business in the building, I should be paying a higher percentage of the typical condo fees, like the other businesses in the building. Interesting. The Administrator responded, explaining that as a B&B is considered a private activity run in one's home, he didn't think that this rule would apply to me. Mister Antagonistic requested that a minute be recorded, describing that the Administrator would verify the rules for a B&B. After-all, he explained, everyone should be expected to follow the same rules.

After three hours, the meeting was still going strong. People were getting anxious to leave, and a couple had already left. I was worried that if more people left, there wouldn't be the majority needed to approve my request.

We finally reached the last agenda item, and most participants were standing and putting their jackets on. I waved to the administrator to remind him of my request. It was just after 21:30, and after a gruelling three and a half hours, the participants reached a quick decision on the last item. Everyone just wanted to go home, and started moving towards the door. The administrator called out, asking them to wait one last minute for my request. I took the next 15 seconds to explain that I would like to place a simple sign beside the entrance, similar to the sign that was already present at the second entrance. Would they approve my request?

There was a quick series of 'yes' from everyone, and I finally had my approval!

4.10
Non fare polemiche - Don't rock the boat

I've been reflecting about writing this entry for a while. I don't like discord, and am less than proud to have missed the social signals. The drama could have been completely avoided if I was more receptive to the advice of friends. It's a good lesson on cultural differences, though.

In Italy, the cultural differences you will encounter in the Service industry will leave you shaking your head. Whether you are visiting a shop, or sitting down to dinner at a restaurant, you are likely to experience examples of both fantastic, genuine and welcoming service, as well as service that is complete crap.

I'm continuously baffled that establishments keep their doors open, even though the quality of their product or their service is horrible. For some cities like Rome, Venice and Florence, the ongoing operations of these 'tourist traps' can be explained by the new hoard of tourists that arrive and depart daily. Why be concerned about quality when tomorrow you know you will be busy with a new crowd of tourists?

In Bologna, where there is less tourism, businesses depend more on their local clients.

During our first year in Bologna, service quality was a regular conversation topic with our friends. That was until we learned our lesson.

Bologna is a VERY social city. Most people don't like to spend their evening at home, alone. Almost every evening of the week, around 7 or 8 pm, there will be a stream of messages with your friends, asking who is in the mood to meet for aperitivo, or maybe even dinner.

Since we spend our days running the B&B at home, if we are not waiting for a guest arrival when evening comes, we have a serious urge go out. After spending the entire day cleaning the B&B, there is little desire to stay at home and make a mess for dinner that will also need to be cleaned. Instead, we go to our favourite hangouts, and pass a few hours chatting with friends over a glass of prosecco, or maybe a spritz aperol.

When the service is crap, everyone is quick to groan. It's common to complain about the poor quality of the wine or cocktails, or the cheap and stale munchies that are provided, or even the higher cost of the drinks compared to other bars close by.

Who doesn't like to gripe?

But if it's a hangout you visit frequently, where you are social with the owner, wouldn't it be better to make a suggestion to the owner, to help improve?

This is where our thinking diverged from many of our Italian friends.

When our friends complain about something that isn't good, I would add that we should mention something to the employee or owner. However, the response from our friends is usually immediate. 'No. Non fare polemiche', they would say, which is a way of saying 'don't cause trouble.'

I heard this response countless times, but why the aversion to speaking up?

After all, in running our B&B, we feel that our guests' comments are very helpful. It's better if they speak-up if they aren't satisfied, so that we can try to fix the issue. For example, when we first opened, we had purchased hairdryers to provide to guests upon request. One guest left a comment on a travel site suggesting that we should leave the hairdryers in their bathrooms, and so we did.

Nowadays, in the world of apps and online travel sites, it's extremely quick and easy for clients to leave a negative comment. A negative comment can damage business almost immediately.

I actually appreciate more those guests who come to me directly with comments or suggestions. They are the ones who are truly concerned with helping us improve and be more successful.

José spent more than 30 years in Switzerland, and I'm from Canada, and we are both comfortable with the idea of making a suggestion regarding quality. It's not possible for owners and employees to be aware of everything, and customer feedback is generally appreciated.

It seems rational, at least in theory.

There is a bar that had opened the previous summer, which we frequented at least 3 or 4 times a week. It's a few minutes' walk from us, and is located on a street where a number of our friends live. The terrace is comfortable in the summer time, and we all got to know the owner well. The space that the owner is renting for the bar is actually owned by the ex of a very good friend of ours. While we are light alcohol drinkers, our friends drink prosecco like it's water, and we would pass hours in the evenings going through at least a couple of bottles.

During the winter months however, we wouldn't visit the bar. We would always choose a different bar with our friends. The reason was simple. The bar had no heating inside. Inside, you would need to keep your winter jacket on, otherwise you would get a chill. While the winters in Bologna aren't arctic like in Canada, the temperature usually ranges between 0 and 5° Celsius, and this isn't a comfortable temperature to be sitting and socializing.

Each time we passed the bar, we saw that there were fewer clients, compared to the crowd that was typical during the summer months. I mentioned to our friends a number of times that we should let the owner of the bar know why we weren't going. I asked, 'Why spend our money at other bars? I would rather spend my money at a bar where we feel at home and are friends with the owner.

Our friends would just respond...'non fare polemiche.'

We had learned from our friend's ex that the owner, I'll call him Sergio for this story, had broken the heating during the renovations to open the bar. He never invested to fix it.

However, it wouldn't take much to solve the problem. A simple, small electric heater could make a huge difference.

Being stubborn, we thought that it couldn't hurt to mention something to Sergio.

One evening, when passing by the bar, we decided to go in and grab a drink. We ordered our usual drinks and went to sit at the back. There was a small group of people having a drink next to us, and all of us were sitting with our winter jackets on. Strangely, Sergio, who was behind the bar, kept the front door fully open. About 10 minutes later, we overheard the group beside us say that there were too cold and were leaving. The bar was now almost empty and we were also getting cold, so we decided to pay and head home.

While we were paying, I said to Sergio 'It's very cold inside.'

'You find it cold?' He asked

'There's no heating, and the door is completely open. We have been sitting with our jackets on'. I replied. 'Some heating could help make people stay longer'.

Sergio pointed to a couple of other bars close by where there were people standing outside smoking. 'Look at those bars. There are a lot of people, and they don't seem to mind the temperature'.

'The people are outside because they can't smoke inside. If people prefer the colder temperature, they have the option to stay outside with their friends. However, people looking to sit inside a bar, are usually expecting a warmer space where they can be comfortable and sit without their winter jackets.'

'I don't think so,' he replied.

Ok, this conversation wasn't making sense. Maybe a more direct approach would help. 'We haven't been coming these last couple of months because it's too cold inside. Our other friends also find it too cold, so we usually choose to go to other bars.'

'You aren't coming here because you prefer to go to different bars, and you just don't want to come here.'

We tried to explain for another couple of minutes, but finally realized that it was pointless. He was not interested in listening. We dropped the topic, said bye and headed home.

A couple months later, the weather was warm enough for a drink on a terrace. We were meeting a friend, and decided to head back to the bar, after not having returned since our conversation.

We sat at a table on the terrace. The bar was busy, both inside and on the terrace. Sergio came by, and we ordered our usual beers. We prefer a darker beer and never order the regular. A few minutes later Sergio returned and quickly deposited three regular beers, then left to go back inside.

José looked at the beers and asked 'Why would Sergio bring regular beers when we had ordered the darker beer?'

'Maybe the darker beer was finished?' I offered.

'Sergio knows that we never drink the regular beer on tap,' José responded. 'If he was out, he could have just mentioned it, and given us the choice to order something else we would like. We should say something'

Thinking back to conversation about the lack of heating, I said, 'I don't think Sergio really cares about hearing our suggestions.'

'It isn't right. We should say something,' José repeated.

We drank the beers, and went to pay.

José decided to speak-up after-all. 'Sergio, we had asked for our usual beer, and you brought us the regular. What happened'?

'I ran out. But I told Adrian that I didn't have any left,' Sergio responded.

That was news to me. Maybe I didn't hear it, or something got lost in translation.

'But we never drink the regular beer. If you had mentioned something we could have ordered something else we like,' José explained.

'Look,' Sergio started raising his voice, 'you see all these people here around the bar? They don't come here causing trouble. They are my friends and they never give me problems. This is my bar, and I don't need you coming here *a fare polemiche*.

'If you don't like my bar, there are plenty other bars you can go to.' Sergio continued. 'And remember when you came a couple months ago saying that you and your friends don't come because it is too cold, you are cowards. Instead of just saying that you don't want to come to my bar, you say that your other friends also have a problem and aren't coming too. You have no courage. I don't need your money. If you don't like my bar, you can go elsewhere.'

We left, and will not be returning.

At least we don't feel alone. A couple months later, he insulted our other friends, who also decided to not return.

We finally understood what our friends meant when they said 'non fare polemiche.' They understood that Sergio didn't care, and were saying that you have a choice: either continue being a customer and don't complain, or just stop frequenting the bar. Speaking up wouldn't change anything.

Not a problem though. As Sergio said, there a many other bars to explore in Bologna, with great drinks, and owners who care about their clients and business. This little push helped us to start exploring the fantastic variety of bars around town.

4.11
Kettle shrimps, anyone?

It's trade-show time, and when a major trade shows rolls into town, things get a little crazy.

A trade show is an important time for businesses in Bologna. Occupancy rates in hotels go up to practically 100%, and restaurants are full every night. These days are the most profitable, and all hotels raise their room rates, including us.

We try not to exaggerate with our rates though, because the guest's perception of value for money can drop like a lead ball, leaving you with lower guest ratings. It's always a bit shocking when we see hotels who may sell rooms in the low season at 80 Euros a night, setting rates at well above 500 Euros per night. There are even B&Bs that rent out rooms with shared bathrooms, who set their rates much higher than ours. Where is the line between making a profit and taking advantage of demand?

A week before the trade show, we had a room blocked that we were reserving for a potential private reservation. Still free, we decided to open the room on one of the major hotel reservation sites. We searched the rates of available hotels on the site, and saw that they were running at more than double our typical trade fair rate. We opened our room at our trade fair rate, and within a half hour the room was reserved.

A couple of days before the arrival of the client, I accessed the reservation to send our typical welcome message, and I noticed that although the reservation was made for one person, there were two names to the reservation. Our room rate for one person is 15% less than for a double occupancy. Were the guests trying to take advantage of the lower rate? I sent our welcome message, and in their reply, they confirmed that they were in two. I responded, asking them to contact the reservation site, as they would need to modify their booking to two people.

A few hours later, I received a call from a representative of the reservation site, who was located in the home country of the guests. The representative explained that the clients felt that the difference in price for two guests compared to one guest was too much, and the representative suggested a different price. Rates are clearly advertised on the site, and people can choose to book or not. When did the rates become negotiable? And when did a prominent international booking site become the negotiation agent for guests?

I said I would think about it. After a quick search on the reservation site, I saw that there were only a few hotels with rooms available. The lowest rate was still double ours, and the highest about 4 times our rate.

I called the reservation site's call centre, somewhat pissed. It felt like they were placing our backs up against the wall. If the clients planned on visiting Bologna, they would need to keep their reservation with us. We were the lowest rate in the city. However, if we didn't agree to their lower rate, they could express their disappointment by leaving negative comments and a poor rating. Regardless, we felt that our rate was fare, and we would be prepared to respond to negative comments. I informed the representative that we were sticking to our rate. The representative said that they would advise the clients.

A short time later, we received a modification for the reservation, indicating two people at the full rate.

On the day of their arrival, we were interested to see who they were and how they would react. They were a friendly younger couple, and they made no mention of the rate during the check-in. As we were showing them their room, they asked if we can provide them with slippers. In each room, we provide complimentary soap and shampoo, as well as tea, coffee and water. While we do not leave other complimentary items, we do have a small stock of items like toothpaste/toothbrushes, shower caps, and yes, even disposable slippers, for those guests who might be in need, or can't do without. We brought the slippers to their room.

The rest of their stay seemed to proceed normally.

On the last night before their checkout, we returned home after aperitivo with friends, and José did his customary check of the hallway, bar and lights before going to bed. He noticed that the electric water kettle, which should be sitting on the bar, was not there. One of the guests took the kettle to their room. Either they had a moment of thoughtlessness, or they were being inconsiderate to the other guests who may want to make a tea. Regardless, we thought we knew in which room the kettle was sitting.

The next morning, the couple needed to leave early, and their breakfast and checkout was quick. After they left, we saw that the kettle was back in its place at the bar. We started to clean their room, and noticed that they had decided to dine in their room the night before. There was a strong odour of shrimps in the room, and many shrimp shells left in their garbage bin.

I went to grab the kettle to pour out any remaining water, and when I opened the lid, an intense odour of shrimps burst out. I was speechless...they bought uncooked shrimps and boiled them in the water kettle! WTF!

The kettle was hopeless. After multiple washes of soap, water and baking soda, and even multi-day baths of vinegar, the water boiled in the kettle always came out 'a la shrimp'. Into the garbage it went, and we were stuck spending 50 Euros to buy a replacement kettle.

After a thorough cleaning of the room, we also couldn't manage to eliminate the smell of shrimps from the room. We were expecting the arrival of repeat clients that evening, and hoped that the smell would be gone before they arrived.

The next morning, during breakfast, we described the kettle story to our repeat guests, and they started laughing. They had noted the eau du shrimp in their room, and couldn't figure out where it was coming from.

At least they were more amused about it than we were.

4.12
Navigating mortgages

So here I am, sitting again in another Notaio's office. No, I am not purchasing a second apartment. I've decided to move my mortgage to a different bank.

While some of my other stories poke fun at some cultural and social differences in Italy, I would like to start by saying that I actually love the Italian mortgage system. A mortgage in Italy is viewed more as a civil right, and not a lengthy prison sentence!

That being said, don't expect to arrive in Italy and be offered a mortgage based on your good credit history...what credit history? Your credit doesn't travel over the ocean with you.

In Italy, a mortgage contract is a long-term relationship. You can even lock-in a fixed interest rate for 30 years, and not just the typical 5-year fixed rate available in North America. This creates more stability in the mortgage market, and in return, the banks expect stability from you. Unless you are wealthy, a bank will usually require that you have a stable job with a permanent job contract, known as a contract that is 'tempo indeterminato'. The bank wants to be assured that you will have a sufficient steady income to make the payments throughout the duration of the mortgage.

Without my 'tempo indeterminato' job contract, I would likely not have been able to get the mortgage needed to buy the apartment for the B&B.

Almost two years have passed since I signed my mortgage contract and apartment purchase contract at the Notaio's office. For my mortgage, I had selected a variable rate, as it was super low compared to the fixed rate. The mortgage product offered by the bank also gave me the option to reconfirm my preference between a variable and fixed rate after two years, and I recently received a letter from my bank to reconfirm.

Reading the letter, I thought 'maybe it's also a good time to negotiate a better rate.' I jumped on the internet and went to www.mutuionline.it[42] (a mortgage is called a 'mutuo' in Italian). It's a great site where you can enter the details of your potential mortgage, either a new or existing mortgage, and it provides you with the latest offers from many major banks. It can also connect you directly to a bank of your choice by sending them your mortgage request and facilitating first contact. After doing a quick test, I saw that a number of banks were offering much lower rates than my current rate. This would translate to a savings of about 100 Euros per month off my current monthly mortgage payment. Strangely though, my bank wasn't one of the ones listed. Two years before, when I was first looking for my mortgage, my bank was offering one of the most competitive rates.

You may be asking, 'why would my bank be willing to change my rate?, and 'why would I think of moving to another bank considering the expensive penalty fees for breaking a mortgage contract?'

This is where it gets good. In 2007-08, the Italian government introduced two specific changes to the laws regarding mortgages and lending (these laws are usually referred to as the 'Legge Bersani'). The first change allows you to make a lump sum payment to your mortgage at any time and for any amount, even the full amount, with no penalty fee. That means that banks cannot restrict extra payments to your mortgage, and you are free to pay off your mortgage as fast as you like.

The second change is even better. It provides the consumer the right to move their mortgage to another bank at any time during their mortgage contract, with no penalty. Yes, you read that right.

I felt somewhat loyal to my current bank, and to the bank representative that had helped me during the start-up of the B&B. However, if I could save significant money, I would seriously considering moving banks.

I decided to call my bank representative.

After getting bounced around the telephone system, I finally reached a human. I asked to speak to my rep, but was informed that she had recently transferred branches to another city, and that the representative who answered the phone would be able to help me.

I briefly described that I had received the letter. I explained that aside from confirming the variable rate option, I was interested in understanding what could be done with the actual rate, seeing that mortgage rates have dropped.

The representative explained that as described in the letter, it is time to confirm the variable rate option. Regarding the actual rate though, she didn't have the 'parameters' to offer a different rate.

Hummm...'maybe something is getting lost in translation', I thought. We have been reliable customers with the bank for a couple years now, and have personal accounts and the B&B account there. Surely the bank would be interested in keeping our business?

Perhaps it would be easier to have this conversation in person. I mentioned to the representative that we would like to visit her in person, and we set a date.

I started to really miss my old bank rep. She was extremely friendly and sincere, and was always ready to help find a solution. We even invited her to our inauguration party, to show our appreciation.

The tone of this new rep on the other hand, seemed uninterested and condescending.

'I'll need to do my homework and go to the appointment prepared with an alternative' I thought. Maybe it would motivate my bank to negotiate.

I went to visit a nearby branch of the bank that was offering the lowest mortgage rate on www.mutuionline.it. I met the branch Director and explained that I was considering moving my mortgage. He was ready to take the information needed to do a preliminary assessment. Perfect! He also confirmed the rate that was advertised online, and mentioned that they would cover the cost of the Notaio's services. Oops! I had forgotten that closing a mortgage deal in Italy requires a Notaio to prepare the contract, oversee the signing, and do the registration. However, if the bank would cover the fees, then there was no need to worry! I asked the Director if there were any other hidden fees to be aware of, and he replied that there would be no other fees.

We completed the preliminary assessment, and the Director listed the documents I would need to give him, if I wanted to proceed with the mortgage request. He also mentioned that they would need to conduct the 'perizia', which is an inspection of the apartment, to confirm the general value of the property. Not a problem. I was really interested to see how much the value may have changed after all the renovations that were done.

> **B&B Owner Tip:** In Canada, when purchasing a house, you can request a mortgage pre-approval, and go into a purchase negotiation knowing that you already have a mortgage approved up to a maximum limit. In Italy however, a bank will not 'pre-approval' a mortgage. They will only do a preliminary calculation to see whether you are likely to be approved for a mortgage, based on information like your pay-check. They won't commit to it though. You will be asked to return after the owner has accepted your offer, and only then will they proceed with the mortgage application. This means you are signing a contract to purchase, and providing a down-payment, without actually knowing if you will be approved for a mortgage. Many real estate agents will also try to tell you that making your offer conditional on a mortgage approval is not the norm, and that the owner would disregard your offer if there is interest from other buyers. You will need to decide how you want to play this game, depending on how much risk you can handle.

I walked out of the bank with a printed preliminary offer, and a 30 day rate guarantee.

We arrived at our appointment with our current bank, and were greeting by the new representative. This new rep had an expression on her face like she just ate something horribly disgusting, which left a bad taste in her mouth. It's normal in Italy to experience what I call the 'service contradiction'. You are likely to encounter either a really friendly and professional service representative, or you will face someone who behaves like they have something better to do than to attend to you.

The representative started by explaining again that I arrived at the two-year mark, and had the option to reconfirm the variable rate, or switch to a predefined fixed rate. I explained that I understood this, but we made the appointment because we were more interested to see if we can renegotiate the actual mortgage rate. We had seen that rates had changed, and were much lower now.

'I don't have the *parameters* to offer a different rate,' the rep repeated the same ambiguous phrase she had previously said over the phone.

'What does that mean,' I asked.

'Your mortgage was obtained for the maximum amount of 80% of the property value, and we cannot offer a different rate for that type of mortgage.' she responded.

'I have been making payments to the principle for 2 years now, so the ratio is no longer 80/20', I replied. 'I have also invested over 100,000 Euros in renovations, redoing everything from electrical wiring to plumbing. This will have increased the actual value of the apartment significantly.'

'It doesn't matter, the mortgage is still viewed as 80/20', she replied. The conversation went back and forth for a few minutes.

'Do you have any other money or investments' she asked.

'No,' I replied. 'My savings were invested in buying and renovating the apartment. Why is that important?'

'If you had, say 100,000 Euros in your bank account, we could consider a more favourable rate. It is your responsibility to demonstrate that you have more leverage to offer'.

I looked at her calmly, controlling the anger that was simmering from her curt and condescending tone. 'It's my responsibility to make my mortgage payments on time, and demonstrate that I am a reliable client. It is also my responsibility to make the best financial decisions for me. I have been to another bank, and already have a really good offer from them. If this bank is not interested in negotiating, I will consider switching to the other bank.'

She looked at me and said 'There is nothing we can offer'.

She hadn't even bothered trying to speak with the branch Director. It didn't matter though. I had noticed that the Director was concentrating on eavesdropping on our not-so-friendly conversation, from his adjacent cubicle, and didn't seem interested in intervening.

That was fine with me. We collected our stuff and walked out.

They lost a customer, and I've just signed a new mortgage contract with a different bank, which will be saving me money.

4.13
Craving a great bolognese meal?

I've mentioned before that one of Bologna's names is 'la turrita', in homage to its towers. However, Bologna is also known by three other names: 'la dotta, la grassa, e la rossa'. 'La dotta' or 'the learned / scholarly' refers to the fact that Bologna is the home of the oldest university in the western world, dating back to 1088. 'La rossa' or 'the red' describes the colour of the bricks used in many if its medieval towers and palazzi. Our friends have also explained that 'red' has a double meaning, and refers to the city's tendency to lean politically to the left, compared with other cities in Italy. Then there's 'la grassa' or 'the fat'. The food is entirely to blame for this name, which is rich and based on the satisfying goodness of pastas, cheeses, prosciutto and more. It's an ongoing challenge to stay slim while living here.

It doesn't help that Bologna has a vast selection of great restaurants to choose from. It's even more satisfying when you have fantastic dining close to home. We continue to add to our list of restaurants nearby, where we eat and also recommend to clients. Our latest addition is just perfect!

It's called <u>Trattoria Da Me</u>[43], and it is located on the picturesque street of Via San Felice. The street is lined with many small specialty and boutique shops, which are protected by the typical Bolognese portici.

It's not a new restaurant. We've passed by it countless times since opening the B&B, but never truly noticed it. In fact, the space has been a restaurant since 1937. It was originally opened by a sister and brother, Nina and Danio, and was called Trattoria da Danio. Now, under the name Trattoria Da Me, Danio's granddaughter Elisa is the chef, and is at the helm.

Both the space and the menu have been redesigned. To our friends, who remember the trattoria in its previous incarnation, Trattoria Da Me provides a fresh, high quality interpretation of Bolognese cuisine.

I can't take credit for the discovery though. It was actually one of our guests who mentioned it. During breakfast each morning, we ask our guests about their previous evening and where they went to eat. A young couple mentioned that they had dined at Trattoria Da Me, and had a delicious meal. They enjoyed it so much, that they reserved for dinner the next night.

One evening, while we were walking down Via San Felice and discussing what we wanted to eat, I remembered our guests' recommendation. We made our way to Trattoria Da Me, and they had a free table.

The renovated decor is classic, clean, and tasteful. It feels like you've been invited to dine in someone's home. If you look closely at the pictures on the walls, you will find old black and white fotos of Danio and the family, as they pass their years in the restaurant.

The servers are very attentive, and ready to offer suggestions on the dishes and wine pairings.

I especially appreciate how Elisa comes out of the kitchen near the end of the dinner, to greet the guests and ask about the meal. After a couple of visits, you already feel like you are with friends.

It was during one of those rounds that we learned from Elisa that her ragù sauce for the tagliatelle is slow cooked overnight on very low heat, for at least 12 hours. The first time I had tasted it I thought 'wow, this is different'. It has a rich and complex flavour. I shared some with José, and his initial reaction was that it must have stewed for a long time.

I admit that I keep ordering the tagliatelle as a starter every time we dine there, and cannot describe first-hand the other pasta dishes. Our friends say that the tortellini in brodo, and other pastas are very tasty.

There is also varied selection for the main course. We love their coniglio (rabbit) medallions! The medallions are de-boned and dressed with the right herbs. They are juicy and full of flavour.

They also offer the traditional Cotoletta alla Bolognese (veal cutlet), which on their menu is called la Petroniana, after Bologna's patron saint San Petronio. Take a cutlet, bread it and fry it, and then add a layer of prosciutto on top, and cover it all with some melted cheese like parmigiano... Yum! It's comfort food, and most Bolognese will say it's a dish best enjoyed during the winter. Again, there is a reason why Bologna is called 'la grassa'!

For desert, I alternate between their pistachio cream topped with chopped pistacchio, and their marscapone with crumble and chocolate sauce. I'm hooked!

We definitely recommend this restaurant to our guests and friends. Their reputation is growing however, and it's becoming necessary to call ahead and make a reservation.

Now that I've raved about Trattoria Da Me, there's another trattoria even closer to our home, and to our hearts. It's called Da Bertino e figli[44]. We eat there regularly, and always recommend it to our guests. While it is not as refined as Trattoria Da Me, it offers quality, home-style cooking that is hearty and satisfying.

It has also preserved the old-school trattoria atmosphere. In fact, it feels like stepping into a time-warp when you enter Da Bertino. The décor hasn't changed much since the original owner Alberto, known as 'Bertino', opened it in 1957. Sadly, Alberto recently passed away. Even though he wasn't able to work in his last few years, he would still pass his days sitting quietly in a corner table, observing the bustle of the staff and clients, right up to his passing. His daughter Claudia and son Stefano continue the tradition that he created, with the support of their mother Anna.

Clients return to Da Bertino for the traditional Bolognese cuisine, which features the typical hand-made pastas like tagliatelle al ragù, tortellini in brodo, lasagne, and tortelloni. There is something very satisfying in the simplicity of the tortelloni, which are like large tortellini, but filled with ricotta cheese instead of meat, and served in a butter and sage sauce that is typical of this region. Sometimes, if I'm really in the mood for pasta, I will order their tortelloni as my first dish, and then their tagliatelle al ragù as my second. I know, I moan about the carbs the day after.

Even though the wife Anna is well past the age of pension, she is still active, and helps by organizing and cleaning tables, and assisting her children and the wait staff. Claudia, the daughter, manages the reservations, seats the guests, and handles the bills. The son Stefano is the master of the cart of boiled meats, or carrello di bolliti misti.

Da Bertino is known for maintaining the tradition of the carrello di bolliti misti. Why throw-out the different meat used to prepare the broth for the tortellini, when you can serve it as a main dish, with some accompanying sauces? Stefano lets you select which meat you would like, or he can prepare a plate for you with a slice of each type. If you have an adventurous palate, ask for 'un po' di tutto', 'a bit of everything', and you can savour meat such as cow tongue and cheek, as well as cotechino and zampone, which are like large sausages made of pork parts.

The family is proud of their business, and around the front desk, you can find photos of the family members over the decades, as well as a collection of newspaper clippings celebrating the restaurant. There's one newspaper article from 1992[45], which always grabs my attention. It features a picture of a much younger Alberto and Stefano, and describes Alberto's secret of Da Bertino's success: 'In cucina solo donne' or 'only women in the kitchen'. Hummmm, my Canadian sensibility has difficulty ignoring the underlying sexism. Our friends however just smile, and don't seem to interpret it like I do. Regardless, we enjoy returning for the welcoming atmosphere and great food!

4.14
Sensitive egos...

We are finally replacing our windows...and have managed to piss-off the window installers.

Of course it would have made more sense to replace the windows during the massive renovations to create the B&B. We would have avoided the mess that needs to be cleaned after each window is installed. We wouldn't have had the workers and material in the way as we continue serving breakfasts and doing check-outs and check-ins. We also wouldn't have had the acrid smell of burnt metal as the workers saw away each of the old frames.

It has definitely been a headache, and also very difficult to organize the installations around a busy reservation schedule.

Unfortunately though, I had reached the very limit of my budget during the renovations (and even exceeded it), and could not squeeze in another 10-15,000 Euros to replace 11 windows.

So now is the time.

The old windows really needed to be replaced. I referred to them as 'windbreakers', as that was the only real function they performed. They were the original aluminium single-pane windows installed in the 60s, when the building was built.

While we are located in Bologna's centre, we are in the north-western part of the circle. Walking around this area, you will note that the architecture is much newer than the typical medieval red brick buildings in other parts of the centre. The reason is that most of the neighbourhood was destroyed by allied bombings during the Second World War. The neighbourhood was then rebuilt, during the Economic Boom period from the 1950s to 1970s. You can still find reminders of the destruction, like the memorial in the last foto of a father and daughter, both pharmacists, who died when their pharmacy was bombed in 1943, on the corner of Via delle Lame and Via Riva di Reno.

The windows in our building are unique. They stand tall, starting from the floor, and almost reaching the ceiling. They are made of two parts, the bottom section that opens on an angle, inwards into the apartment, and the upper section that runs from the right to the left, rolling right into a space in the left side wall.

While they let a lot of light in, they do little to insulate against the heat and cold. During the winter, if the shutters are closed at night, the windows will be completely covered in condensation in the morning. The single pane also doesn't insulate from street noise. We are lucky to be in a quiet neighbourhood. Nevertheless, the city schedules its garbage pick-up and street cleaning during the week, usually after midnight. These activities can wake-up the guests, and some guests have even suggested in their comments to replace the windows.

So for everyone's comfort and peaceful sleep, including our own, we contacted a couple of Infissi providers to get some quotes ('infissi' is a term used to refer to fixed window and door installations).

We eventually selected the provider who actually offered a more expensive quote.

It would have been way too costly to create windows that rolled into the space in the walls, like the original ones. Instead, we focused on searching for modern windows, which open the standard way, into the apartment. We were worried though that the thick PVC frames typical of newer windows would reduce the amount of light entering into the apartment. The company we selected offered windows with thinner frames. Coincidentally, it was the same company that supplied the doors to our B&B during the major renovation.

The Sales Representative visited our apartment to examine the existing windows, and discuss our needs. We then went to the store's showroom to inspect the actual window model. We were also very interested in glass that had greater sound-proofing for the bedrooms, and added it to our order, at an extra cost.

We asked the Representative how soon the windows could be delivered. It wouldn't be possible to install the windows when the rooms are occupied by guests, and we had a long weekend of 5 days blocked a couple months away. We explained that we would like to schedule the installation during that long weekend.

He replied that the timing shouldn't be a problem.

Perfect! I signed the contract and made the first payment.

B&B Owner Tip: Check with your Commercialista to learn about any tax rebate or other government programs related to energy saving improvements. Italy has some very favourable rebates that can be spread across multiple years of your tax returns. Note though, to take advantage of the rebates, you will need more than just the invoices from the company providing the services/products. You are required to process the payment of the invoices at the bank, where they will register the invoice and company details, as well as your codice fiscale (social insurance number). Payments can only be made via bank transfer. No cash payments are allowed!

It was wishful thinking to think that the windows would arrive on time. Deadlines can become an abstract concept in Italy, and we hit one delay after another.

If you want to get something done, be prepared to act as the project manager. Even though we were dealing with one company, each time I called or sent an email, I would be given the number of a different employee that I would need to contact directly to arrange the next step.

After signing the contract, I was advised to call the technician who specialized in taking the exact measurements that would be sent to the window manufacturer. I gave him a call, and had to juggle with his calendar to find a suitable date for him to visit. He came to take the measurements, but then had to reconfirm the numbers and discuss some complications with us. For example, he realized that we couldn't use regular sized handles because there wasn't enough space between the window and the original shutters to be able to open and close the shutters. The only solution offered was to use removable handles.

The order was finally placed, and I was told that they would call when the windows arrived. Almost two months passed, and no call came. I decided to call to ask what was happening, and was told that the windows had just arrived and that they were planning to call me…what a coincidence.

I was then provided the number of the window installers, whom I had to call to discuss their availability for a first visit. We were now well passed the original long weekend that was blocked, but there was a shorter long weekend of 4 days coming up.

When the installers arrived to discuss the installation details, they casually mentioned that they do not work weekends. This complicated everything!

Aside from the weekend that we blocked for us, there weren't any other days where the B&B was completely free of guests. We would need to make arrangements to install the windows based on the separate availability of each room.

As they were examining the existing windows, the installers also told us that it was going to be VERY complicated to remove the frames of the existing windows and set up a new frame, and that we should plan for at least one day to install each window. We had 11 windows to replace!

Then they started shaking their heads while inspecting the windows. 'Replacing the windows will be dangerous, as there isn't a barrier to protect us or material from falling out,' they said. 'We don't feel secure doing the installations.'

'What do you mean? Both the Sales Representative and the Technician were here and inspected the windows, and they never mentioned any safety issue.'

'The form of the windows won't let us set up the typical safety barriers. We will call the Geometra, and he will need to find a solution'.

Really? Now a Geometra needs to be involved?

A Geometra is a seudo architect profession in Italy - with limitations. He or she can get involved in small-scale renovation projects, but does not have the authority to manage larger construction projects where the safety of people is concerned.

After a visit by the Geometra, and an exchange of drawings sent via email, we settled on a solution. During the installation of each window, they would need to drill a couple of holes in the structure outside the window, place a metal frame on each side, and then slide a wooden panel, to prevent the possibility of something or someone from falling out the open space.

More than 3 months had passed since we signed the contract. At this point, you may be asking - why didn't we freak out from the poor service and coordination? In the end, we still need to rely on each of them to do their work, and do it well. In Italy, you can usually achieve more with honey, than with a temper. If you offend or create a confrontational relationship, you could find yourself facing larger obstacles, and shoddy work.

So I continued to breath, and keep my project manager hat on.

The material was finally delivered and the work was ready to start.

The two window installers were a very interesting pair. They were a father and son team. The father was 71 years old and still going strong. He was also more diplomatic, compared to his son's expressive personality. They were great installers, very methodical and they had a really good eye for quality...for the most part.

The part that wasn't done well involved two windows in one of the bedrooms. The two windows weren't fully level after their installation.

When we tried to close the windows, they wouldn't line up to the frame properly and we needed to press the window against the frame at a couple of points, to be able to close the handle.

Well, they installed nine out of eleven windows perfectly. Mistakes happen.

Thinking back to the day that they installed those two windows, I remembered that they arrived earlier than usual, and sent us a message to say that they would need to leave early. That evening, the Italian soccer team was playing in the European championships, and all Italians would be glued to their television screens. In fact, when the Italian team plays, the entire city goes silent. You can usually follow the results by the punctuation of massive moans or cheers that rise throughout the city during a game.

Considering that the installers were able to mount nine windows properly, it looks like they may have rushed through their work that day.

The installers arrived one last day, to finish the installations. After we greeted them, José mentioned that there was a problem with the two windows. They weren't convinced. José took them to the room to show them, and the father looked to the son, and said under his breath, 'Didn't you check that they were level before finishing the installation?'

The son frowned, and said he would come back to the windows after completing the work on the other windows.

About an hour later, the son starting talking to José, saying that there was nothing wrong with the two windows.

'The windows are installed against the existing walls of the building,' he explained. 'If the building walls aren't level, then of course the windows wouldn't be. You will just need to explain to your guests where to push to be able to close the windows.'

Really? They were able to install nine windows properly, and it's the fault of the walls of the building that two windows don't close?

Did I mention that José used to do carpentry, and specifically worked on door and window installations?

'Look,' José said, 'I was a carpenter. When installing windows, the window needs to be tested once it's in place, to make sure that everything is level and it closes properly. There is always enough space left between the window and frame to make the small adjustments needed until everything is level. Even if a building's wall isn't straight, the window is adjusted to the frame to make sure it can close properly.'

'Everyone says that they used to be a carpenter, but it doesn't mean that they actually did the work and know what they are talking about,' the son replied.

'Well in my case it's true,' José responded. 'The windows can't be left like they are. They need to be fixed.'

The son continued his rant, saying it wasn't possible to adjust if the walls aren't straight.

He was pissed. The father tried to calm him, but the son stormed off.

Over the next couple of hours, he huffed around while completing the finishing work on the other windows. He eventually returned with his father to the bedroom, and re-adjusted the two windows until they closed properly.

Mistakes can happen any time. It usually takes less energy to just accept the problem and fix it. In Italy though, I find it rare to hear someone admit their error. It's even rarer to hear someone utter the word 'sorry'.

A couple of days later, we were speaking with our plumber, who was inspecting our air-conditioning units, as they weren't functioning well. We described the drama about the windows and he laughed. He explained that he visited a client a couple weeks before, who had a water leak in his bathroom. The plumber found the leak, and saw that it was a result of a mistake he made during the original installation. He explained this to the client and said he would repair the problem. The client looked at him absolutely dumbfounded. When the plumber asked what was wrong, the client responded that he never had the experience where a professional admitted a mistake and took responsibility. He said that he was prepared for a lengthy argument where the plumber would make fantastical explanations to lay blame elsewhere, and then expect extra money to make the repairs.

While honey will get people working, sometimes you also need to hold your ground, to get things done right.

4.15
A little visit from the city

We received a visit from a city official yesterday. When someone rings the bell to your door, and presents themselves as a representative from the city who is there to deliver a notice, your first reaction is automatic - 'oh no, what's wrong!'

'I am here to deliver this **verbale**,' he explained. 'You are being charged a fine by the city.'

'A fine? What for?' José took the verbale, an official city document that's like a oversized ticket.

'The city found a bag of garbage that belonged to you, which was left outside against city regulations.'

'What do you mean?' José was confused. He looked at the document, and the reason written for the fine was:

'Abbandono rifiuti in modo non conforme al regolamento comunale.'

In other words, *'the abandonment of garbage in a method that does not conform to city regulations'*. Beneath this sentence, there was a paragraph explaining that an inspection was made of a blue sack containing paper, which was abandoned on public ground, beside our building door. From the inspection, they found information that demonstrated we were the owners of the sack.

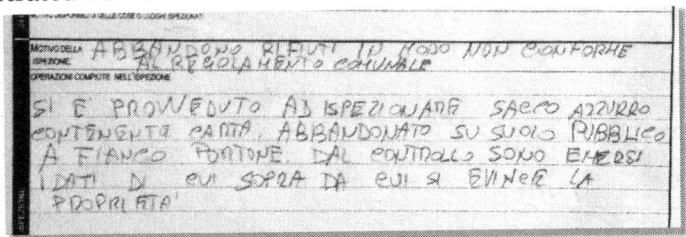

The cost of the fine – 50 Euros.

'We always take our garbage out according to the weekly schedule,' José was astonished.

Last year, the city of Bologna invested a lot of money and work to revamp the garbage collection system in the centre. Before the change, there were large garbage bins sitting along many streets in the centre, where everyone would dump all of their garbage. There was no recycling program. The city removed most of these large garbage bins, and excavated to replace them with pairs of smaller bins. These new bins have smaller receptacles to throw the bags, and the actual deposits are hidden beneath ground level. One bin is for aluminium cans and glass, and the other for organic waste.

What about general waste? The city now comes only once a week to pick up garbage bags with general waste. In our area, it's on Monday nights. Everyone is expected to leave their garbage bags outside their building doors between 8pm and 10pm, and the city collectors come to pick up the garbage any time after 10pm. Sometimes the trucks come well after midnight.

The city also organizes a separate weekly collection for plastics and papers. Tuesday night is our night, where we leave the sacks outside the building door for the plastic and paper pick-up.

The whole system is a great way to encourage people to be disciplined in separating their garbage and recycling. If you don't want your apartment to smell like rotting waste, you are going to separate out the organic, and dump it regularly in one of the receptacles on the street. Removing the large garbage bins on the streets has also improved the look - and smell - of the city.

'We always have bags of both plastic and paper to recycle every week. We bring all the sacks out at the same time, Tuesday evenings,' José repeated. 'We would never have brought out a sack of paper at a different time or different day. It's obvious that the collectors missed a sack.'

We actually remember that about a month before, we noticed a blue paper recycling sack sitting outside the entrance of our building, the day after the garbage collection. We commented to each other that the collectors had left something behind, again. It's not the first time that they didn't collect all the garbage.

It's the first time though, that it was one of our bags. The problem is, you don't know whose bag is whose. Everyone uses the same recycling bags, which we are required to pick-up at the city's office. There is the standard yellow sack for plastics, and the blue sack for paper.

If we had known that there was a garbage police that goes around opening up abandoned bags, to see who they belong to and to give them a fine, we would have looked inside the sack to see if it was one of our own bags.

That doesn't ignore the fact though that we are being fined for an infraction that we didn't commit!

>**Traveller Tip**: The Police system in Italy can be very confusing. I haven't yet invested the time to research and understand all the roles of the different police. There are the Polizia di Stato (State Police), Polizia Penitenziaria (Penitentiary Police), Corpo Forestale dello Stato (State Forestry Corps), Guardia di Finanza (Finance Guard), and the Carabinieri (a military organisation). Don't forget the actual military, as well as the municipal police. Sometimes you can find representatives from two or three of these organisations patrolling the same area, like a Piazza. Why they all need to be there, and how they separate who-does-what continues to be a mystery to me, and to the Italians that I ask.
>
>If you are visiting Italy, there are a couple of points to remember. It's normal for the police to make spot checks, where they stop people and ask for identification. You should always have a formal government identification with you, in case you are stopped.

Also, the Guardia di Finanza are generally proactive in patrolling to prevent fraud and tax evasion. If you've visited Italy, you may have noticed that when making a purchase, even for a simple espresso at a bar, the cashier will stubbornly ask you to take your receipt with you. The reason is that the Guardia di Finanza may be making spot inspections. As you leave the store, they will ask you to show the receipt for your purchase. If you do not have a receipt, the store will face strict penalties.

'Why should we pay a fine, when it was the collectors who didn't do their job?' José questioned. 'Also, how can the city fine us, when they can't confirm when the bag was left outside the door of the building?'

The city official seemed sympathetic. 'Listen,' he said, 'there is a way to dispute the fine. But the process can be complicated and lengthy. To save you all the effort and stress, it might be better to just pay the 50 Euros.'

He said good-bye, and left to make his next visit.

The injustice of the fine was frustrating. We pay the city taxes for the garbage collection, and we follow the rules perfectly. Then, when the nightly garbage collectors don't do their job, we are fined for their sloppy work?

That afternoon, I researched the process for disputing a fine on the city's website[46]. There are a couple of avenues. However, they ask for: '...*difensivi e documenti comprovanti l'estraneità ai fatti accertati...*'

Essentially they require a person to demonstrate proof to counter the **verified facts**.

That's great. All the city has is one of our blue paper recycling sacks. They have no proof of when we left it there, and whose fault it was that the sack is there after the collection day. Regardless, they can justify giving us a fine, and we are then required to dispute it with proof.

José was angry. He handed me the verbale, and asked me to pay the fine via our online banking, so that he can file the paper and not have to look at it again.

The next day, we were discussing the fine with our friends, and one explained that the same thing has happened a couple of times at their office. They decided to stop separating and leaving out the recycling sacks. Instead they just place everything together in the general garbage pick-up.

An interesting paradox. The city invests to create a comprehensive recycling system, and then penalizes the public for issues related to its service, which discourages people to actually recycle.

Italy is a love-it or leave-it country. You need to be flexible, and accept the craziness along with the passion. They balance each other out, and maybe they even need each other to coexist. There are times when a situation will leave you bewildered, or even just pissed. It's better though to just laugh about it with friends over some good wine. If you fight against the craziness, you will be the one to lose in the end.

One thing is certain. We will never place another piece of paper into the paper recycling sack that can identify us.

4.16
The next chapter

The couple enjoying their breakfast are really friendly and chatty. Interested in hearing about our Bed and Breakfast, they've been asking questions like what inspired the concept, do we run it as a registered business, what is our typical occupancy and length of stay... and more

They are from Turkey, and coincidentally, own a couple of hotels that total a few hundred rooms. I wonder what they think of our little B&B after staying the night. How do we compare to the experience they offer at their hotels?

'Have you considered expanding the B&B,' the husband asked?

'We've talked about it, but haven't really considered it seriously,' I replied.

'You could open more locations in Bologna, or even in another city,' he suggested.

'It's an idea we've discussed. In Bologna, we would need to organize it in another apartment that is very close, otherwise we would waste too much time moving between apartments,' I explained. 'To open a B&B in another city, it would need to be at the right price, and in a city that we love. It would be a challenge though to manage the multiple locations while maintaining the quality.'

'I control the quality because I am doing the work,' José explained. 'Our guests appreciate how clean the rooms and bathrooms are kept. One guest even said that it was the first time that she felt comfortable walking barefoot in a hotel room.'

'I think that both of you can manage to keep a high quality standard in more than one location, with the right people of course,' the husband encouraged.

Expanding is a tempting idea, but would we be ready? For now, we are content that we've reached a comfortable routine.

José submitted his resignation at the end of his sabbatical and is dedicated to maintaining the B&B. In the end, the decision wasn't a dramatic event. Rather, he mentioned that he was ready to finalize the change, and drafted his resignation letter. He called his boss and communicated his decision. We had a couple weeks of vacation planned, and closed the B&B to head to the beach for some rest. Instead of returning to Switzerland to restart his work after the vacation, we returned to Bologna and continued running the B&B.

What's next? I'm not sure.

I don't like to be idle. I especially like a challenge. Writing this book has been a perfect outlet for a time. Aside from feeling compelled to document these stories over the last few years, describing my experiences has given me focus.

Maybe now I need a new idea to seize my curiosity and push me into a new chapter.

If it's as dramatic and entertaining as this journey has been to open a Bed and Breakfast in Bologna, I can't wait to share my experiences with you.

5 Recipes

5.1
Paola Pini's Tortellini in Brodo

Ingredienti - Ingredients

Brodo – Soup
- 5 litri di acqua – litres of water
- 1Kg di carne composta da – of meat made up of:
    - Doppione – Short Rib
    - Punta di petto – Short Plate / Stewing Beef
    - 1/4 di gallina - hen
    - Un pezzetto di codone - sirloin
- in più un bell'osso di manzo con midollo – also add a nice beef bone with marrow
- un gambo di sedano, una cipolla, una carota – one celery stalk, one onion, one carrot
- sale - salt

Sfoglia – Pasta Dough
- 400g di farina '00' – this flour type refers to finely ground flour, you could use all purpose flour
- 4 uova – eggs
- ½ cucchiaio di olio d'olive se impasti la sfoglia in un mixer – ½ tablespoon of olive oil if you mix the ingredients in a food processor

Ripieno di Tortellini – Tortellini Filling
- 400g arista di maiale o braciolo di maiale – pork tenderloin or rack of pork (400g without bone)
- 200g mortadella tagliata grossa – mortadella cut thick
- 50g prosciutto di parma in una sola fetta – single slice of prosciutto
- 200g parmigiano reggiano di 30 mesi – Parmesan Reggiano aged 30 months
- ½ cucchiaio di burro – ½ tablespoon of butter
- 1 piccolo cucchiaino di noci moscate – small teaspoon of nutmeg
- 2 uova – eggs

Istruzioni - Directions

Brodo – Soup (Preparazione la sera prima - Prepare the evening before)

 Lava la carne e pulisce le verdure. Wash the meat and vegetables.	 In una pentola, aggiunge 5 litri di acqua freddo. Add 5 litres of cold water to a large stock pot.
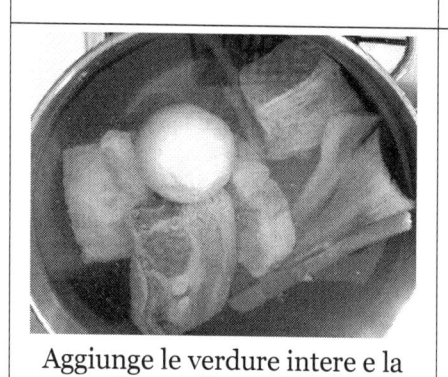 Aggiunge le verdure intere e la carne (manzo), e farla cuocere per circa 20 minuti. Add the whole vegetables to the water, as well as the beef, and cook for about 20 minutes.	 Aggiunge la gallina. Add the hen.

Aggiunge una bella manciata di sale.

Add a palm-full of salt.

Riduce il fuoco e fa bollire lentamente.

Reduce the heat and let boil slowly.

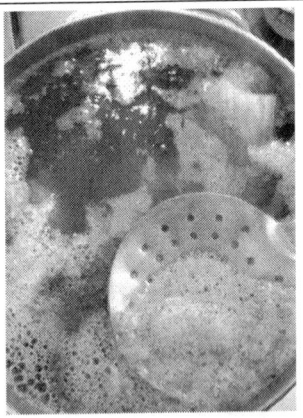

Con la schiumarola togliere la schiuma che viene a galla finchè il brodo rimane limpido.

With a perforated spoon, remove the foam that appears at the top, until the broth is clear.

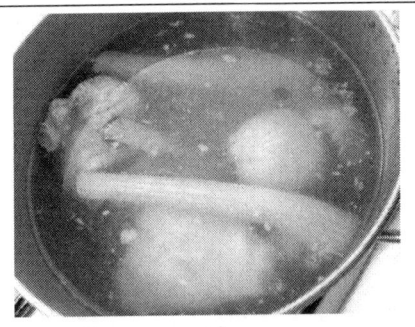

Cuoce per circa 2 ore, controllando la cottura carne con forchetta.

Cook for about 2 hours, controlling that the meat has been cooked with a fork.

Toglie la carne e verdure dal brodo.
Remove the vegetables and meat from the broth.

Trasferisce il brodo in un contenitore e mette nel frigo per la notte.
Put the broth into a container and store in the fridge overnight.

Sfoglia – Pasta Pastry

Nota: Invece di seguire i primi tre direzione per creare l'impasto usando un mixer, può anche fare a mano. Per fare l'impasto a mano, aggiunge la farina sul tagliere, creando una piccola colina. Crea un fosso nella cima della colina di farina, e aggiunge le uova nel fosso. Poco a poco, mescola la farina dentro il fosso di uova, finche gli ingredienti sono tutti mescolati e il risultato è un impasto che può maneggiare.

Note: Instead of using a mixer, you can create the dough by hand. Create a little hill of flour on a wooden cutting board. Make a crater at the top of the hill, and add the eggs to the crater. Slowly, bring the flour into the eggs, and continue mixing until the ingredients are completely mixed, and you have a dough that you can knead.

Aggiunge la farina a un mixer.
Add the flour to a food processor.

Aggiunge le uova.
Add the eggs.

Mescola un po', finché la farina e uova diventano un impasto abbastanza solido per maneggiare. Può anche aggiungere mezzo cucchiaio di olio d'oliva per aiutarla a mescolare.

Mix the ingredients for a bit, until they become a dough that you can knead. You can also add half a tablespoon of olive oil to help mix the ingredients.

Aggiunge un po' di farina a un tagliere.

Add a bit of flour to a wooden cutting board.

Prende l'impasto dal mixer e crea una palla.

Take the dough from the mixer and mould it into a ball.

Lavora l'impasto usando il palmo della mano, premendo da giù in su.

Knead the dough, using the palm of your hand by pressing from down to up.

Piega l'impasto verso di se, e continua a lavorare l'impasto finche è liscio e flessibile.

Fold the dough towards you, and continue the kneading motion, until the dough reaches a smooth and flexible consistency.

Mette l'impasto in una ciotola, coprendolo con uno straccio secco.

Place the dough in a bowl and cover with a dry wash cloth.

Ripieno di Tortellini – Tortellini Filling

Avrà bisogno di un macinatore per macinare l'ingredienti del ripieno. Questo versione manuale funziona benissimo.

You will need a grinder to grind the ingredients for the tortellini filling. This manual grinder works perfectly.

Macina la mortadella e il prosciutto, e mette gli ingredienti in una ciotola.

Grind the mortadella and prosciutto, and place the ingredients in a bowl.

Scioglie il burro in una padella, e aggiunge l'arista di maiale.

Melt butter in a frying pan and add the pork tenderloin.

Cuoce la carne sul fuoco media. Toglie la carne dal fuoco quando è appena cotta.

Cook on medium heat, and remove once the meat is no longer red in the middle.

Macina la carne e l'aggiunge agli altri ingredienti.

Grind the meat and add to the other ingredients.

Aggiunge un cucchiaino di noci moscate.

Add a teaspoon of nutmeg.

Grattugia il parmigiano.
Grate the parmesan.

Aggiunge il parmigiano grattugiato.
Add the grated parmesan.

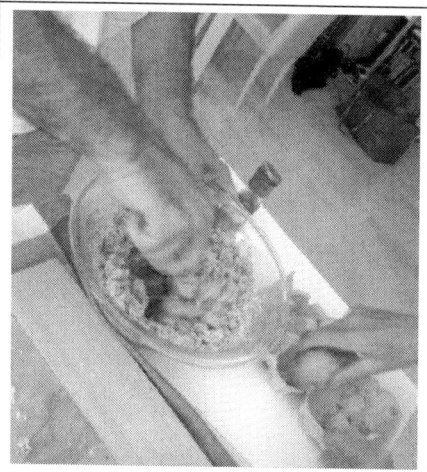

Aggiunge le uova, e mescola tutto, anche con le mani per essere sicuro che è tutto mescolato bene.

Add the eggs, and then mix all the ingredients, even using your hands, until all is well mixed.

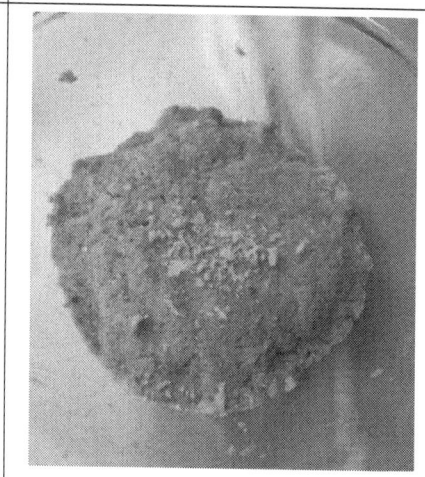

Tortellini

Si può usare una macchina per pasta, per stendere l'impasto.

You can use a pasta maker to roll out the pasta dough.

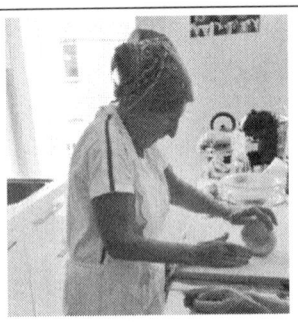

Prende l'impasto dalla ciotola e taglia un pezzo, la misura del palmo della mano. Rimette e copre il resto del'impasto nella ciotola.

Take the dough from the bowl and cut off a chunk, the size of the palm of your hand. Place the remaining dough back in the bowl and cover it.

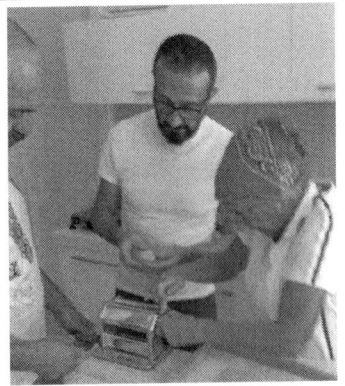

Mette l'impostazione della macchina al più grande spessore, e preme l'impasto traverso la macchina.

Set the machine at the widest width, and pass the dough through the press.

Piega l'impasto, e lo passa traverso la macchina circa 7-8 volte, piegandolo prima ogni volta, finché è liscio e uniforme.

Fold the dough, and pass it through the press another 7-8 times, folding it first each time, until the dough is smooth and uniform.

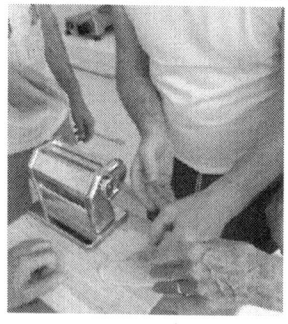

Mette l'impostazione della macchina al prossimo passo di spessore, e passa l'impasto una volta.

Set the machine at the next step of smaller width, and pass the dough through one time.

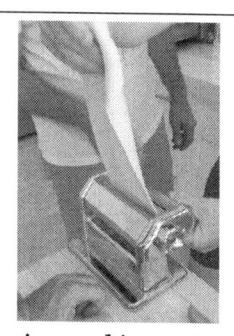

Continua ad impostare la macchina ad ogni passo di spessore, passando l'impasto una volta ad ogni passo, finche l'impasto è passato al spessore più ristretto.

Continue setting the machine at step reducing the width, and at each step, pass the dough through one time, until you passed the dough through at the step with the thinnest width.

Al fine arriva ad ottenere un lungo, fino strato d'impasto. Taglia l'impasto in due, e allungare ogni foglia su un tagliere.

At the end, you will have a long thin stretch of pasta dough. Cut it into two, and place the two sheets onto a wooden cutting board.

Usando un tagliapasta, taglia la foglia in una rete di quadrati, ogni quadrato circa 4-4.5cm per 4-4.5cm.

Using a pastry cutter, cut the sheet into a grid of squares, with each square about 4-4.5cm by 4-4.5 cm.

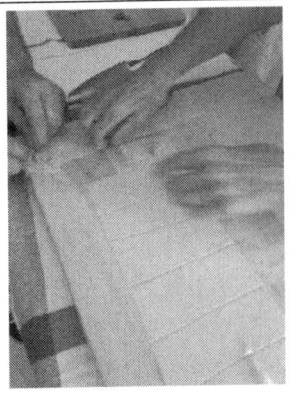

Prende una piccola palina d'impasto del ripieno, e mette nel centro di un quadrato.

Make a small ball of the tortellini filling, and place it in the centre of one of the pasta squares.

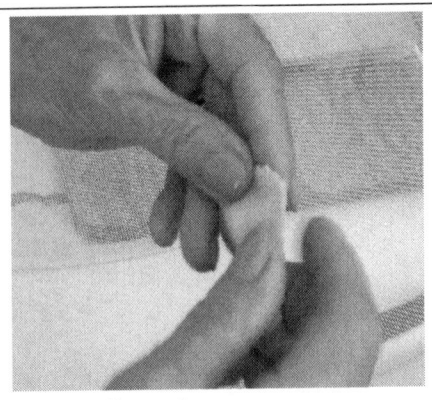

Piega il quadrate per creare un triangolo, con la palina d'impasto nel centro, e preme i lati del triangolo per chiudere i bordi.

Fold the square into a triangle, with the ball of filling in the centre, and press along the edges, to seal the edges.

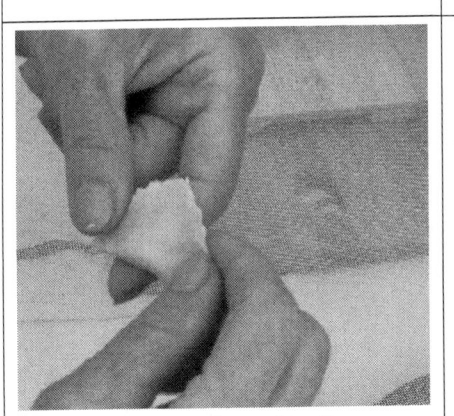

Mette il triangolo sul indice, con la cima del triangolo puntando nella direzione opposta del punto del indice.

Place the triangle on your pointer finger, with the tip of the triangle pointing away from your finger tip.

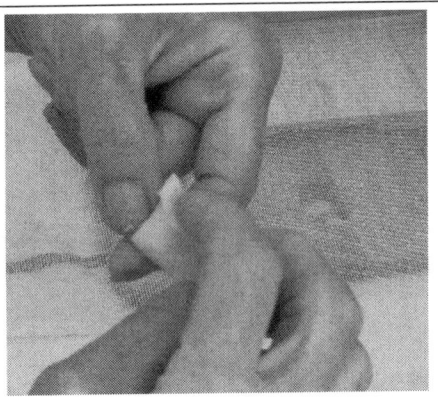

Piega il punto del triangolo verso il punto dell'indice.

Fold the point of the triangle towards your finger tip.

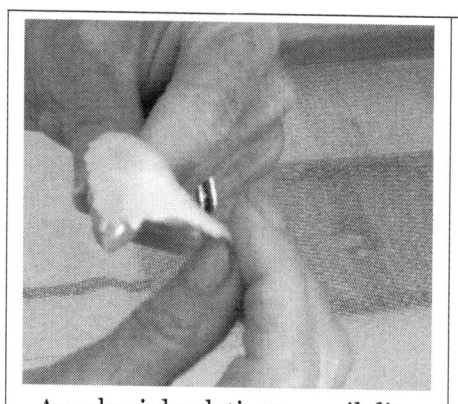

Avvolge i due lati attorno il dito per creare un anello.

Wrap the two sides of the triangle around your finger to create a ring.

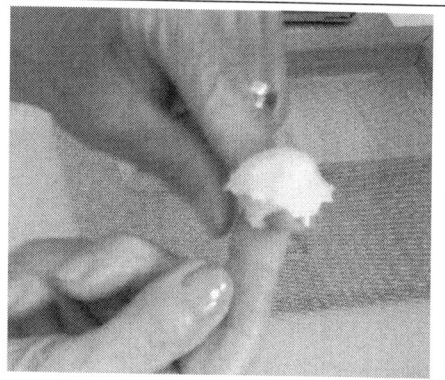

Preme l'incrocio dei due lati per chiudere l'anello.

Press the two sides where they meet, to close the ring.

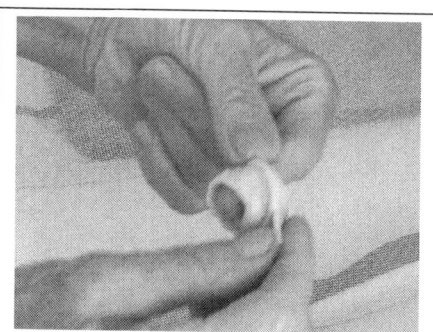

Il primo tortellino è fatto.

Your first tortellino is done.

Continua il processo per creare i tortellini, mettendoli su una seccapasta.

Continue the process of making the tortellini, placing the finished ones on a pasta drying rack.

Si può anche metterli su un tagliere se non ha una seccapasta.

You can also place them on a wooden cutting board if you do not have a drying rack.

Nota: Si può anche congelare i tortellini. Per essere sicuro che i tortellini non si incollano nel congelatore, stendere i tortellini sopra una foglio di carta di forno su un vassoio di metallo o di plastica, e mette il vassoio nel congelatore per un 1-2 ore. Poi, prende il vassoio dal congelatore, e mette i tortellini in un sacchetto di plastica. Chiude il sacchetto e rimetterlo nel congelatore. Per cucinarli, fa bollire il brodo, e mette i tortellini direttamente nel brodo, ancora congelato. Non scongelare i tortellini prima. Di solito ci vuole meno tempo, circa 5 minuti, per essere pronti.

Note: You can also freeze the tortellini. To make sure that they do not stick together, lay the tortellini on a sheet of wax paper on a metal or plastic tray, and place the tray in the freezer for 1-2 hours. Remove the tray and place the tortellini in a plastic ziplock bag. Place the back in the freezer. To cook, simply bring the broth to a boil and add the tortellini, still frozen. Do not defrost them first. Usually it takes less time, around 5 minutes, for the tortellini to be ready.

Preparare Tortellini in Brodo – Preparing the Tortellini in Broth

 Prende il brodo dal frigo. Remove the broth from the fridge.	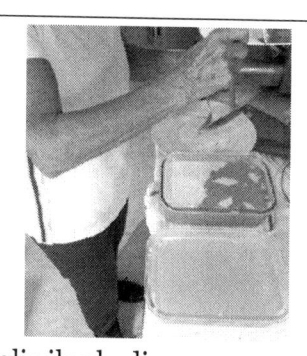 Toglie il velo di grasso rappreso che affiora in superficie. Remove the layer of fat that has formed at the top of the broth.
 Aggiunge il brodo in una pentola e farla bollire. Poi, agginge i tortellini (circa 100-150 grammi per persona) all'acqua. Cuoce i tortellini per circa 8 minuti. Bring the broth to a boil in a pot, and then add the tortellini (about 100-150 grams per person). Cook the tortellini for about 8 minutes.	 Serve i tortellini, aggiungendo un po' di parmigiano al gusto. Serve the tortellini, adding a bit of grated parmesan to taste.

6 Endnotes

1. *È arrivato «big snow», strade in tilt Treni, ritardi fino a 100 minuti.* Corriere di Bologna. 06/02/2015. http://corrieredibologna.corriere.it/bologna/notizie/cronaca/2015/6-febbraio-2015/arrivato-big-snow-strade-tilt-chiusi-marconi-a13-230943833571.shtml
2. Official Ticket Reservation Site to visit the Cenacolo Vinciano (Leonardo da Vinci's Last Supper) http://www.vivaticket.it/?op=cenacoloVinciano
3. Arcigay. http://www.arcigay.it/
4. L'associazione radicale Certi Diritti. http://www.certidiritti.org/
5. *Milano, permesso di soggiorno dalla questura al coniuge gay.* La Repubblica Milano. 31/08/2012. http://milano.repubblica.it/cronaca/2012/08/31/news/milano_permesso_di_soggiorno_dalla_questura_al_coniuge_gay-41781513/?refresh_ce

    Milano, sposato all'estero con italiano: la questura dà il 'soggiorno' a un serbo. Il Fatto Quotidiano. 02/09/2012. http://www.ilfattoquotidiano.it/2012/09/02/milano-questura-permesso-di-soggiorno-al-marito-sposato-allestero-di-italiano/340362/

    E' sposato con un italiano gay: gli danno permesso di soggiorno. Libero Quotidiano. 31/08/2012. http://www.liberoquotidiano.it/news/italia/1069338/E--sposato-con-un-italiano-gay---gli-danno-permesso-di-soggiorno.html
6. Gelato di Capra. http://gelatodicapra.it/
7. La Cremeria della Grada. https://www.facebook.com/lacremeria.dellagrada/
8. Bologna, Lavandaie in via Riva di Reno. Genus Bononiae. http://collezioni.genusbononiae.it/products/dettaglio/8618
9. Mercato delle Erbe. http://www.mercatodelleerbe.eu/
10. Pescheria del Pavaglione. http://www.pescheriadelpavaglione.it/
11. Osteria del Sole. http://www.osteriadelsole.it/
12. Tribunale di Bologna. http://www.tribunale.bologna.giustizia.it/pubblicita-legale
13. Under the Tuscan Sun. Audrey Wells. Buena Vista Pictures. 2003.

14	Portale Notarile Notaio.org. www.notaio.org
15	Cremeria Funivia. http://www.cremeriafunivia.com/
16	La Sorbetteria Castiglione. http://www.lasorbetteria.it/
17	Pellegrino 1936 – Antica Gelateria Artigianale. https://www.facebook.com/GelateriaPellegrino1936/
18	Casa.it S.r.l. http://www.casa.it/
19	Immobiliare.it. http://www.immobiliare.it/
20	La scienza in cucina e l'arte di mangiar bene. Artusi, Pellegrino. 1891.
21	Comune di Forlimpopoli. La scienza in cucina e l'arte di mangiar bene. http://www.pellegrinoartusi.it/il-libro/
22	Pasta Fresca Naldi. https://www.facebook.com/pastafrescanaldi/
23	Accademia Italiana della Cucina. http://www.accademiaitalianacucina.it/it/content/rag%C3%B9-alla-bolognese
24	Bologna Welcome. http://www.bolognawelcome.com/home/scopri/percorsi/cultura/bologna-delle-torri/
25	Bologna Welcome. http://www.bolognawelcome.com/home/scopri/luoghi/architettura-e-monumenti/edifici-e-vie-storiche/i-portici-di-bologna/
26	Biblioteca Salaborsa. http://www.bibliotecasalaborsa.it/cronologia/bologna/1862/2352
27	Didasco Associazione Culturale. http://www.didasconline.it/didasco/
28	Comune di Bologna. http://www.storiaememoriadibologna.it/certosa
29	Comune di Bologna. http://www.storiaememoriadibologna.it/certosa/maserati-alfieri-514641-persona
30	Ornella Stingo. http://www.ornellastingo.com/
31	Carusi Snc. http://www.carusi.it/
32	Santuario del Corpus Domini. http://www.santuariocorpusdomini.it/

33 Felsina, Bononia Bologna. http://www.sselmi.net/santa.html
34 La Repubblica.it. http://ricerca.repubblica.it/repubblica/archivio/repubblica/2007/12/22/la-culla-dei-bastardini-piu-amata-del.html
35 Bologna Welcome. http://www.bolognawelcome.com/en/home/discover/places/architecture-and-monuments/religious-places/complesso-di-san-michele-in-bosco/
36 Servizio Sanitario Regionale Emilia-Romagna: Istituto Ortopedico Rizzoli di Bologna. http://www.ior.it/
37 Le Serre dei Giardini. http://leserre.kilowatt.bo.it/contatti/
38 Cremeria Santo Stefano. https://www.facebook.com/CremeriaSantoStefano/
39 Parlamento Italiano. Legge 29 marzo 2001, n. 135 "Riforma della legislazione nazionale del turismo". http://www.camera.it/parlam/leggi/01135l.htm
40 Regione Emilia-Romagna. http://imprese.regione.emilia-romagna.it/turismo
41 Regione Emilia-Romagna. http://imprese.regione.emilia-romagna.it/turismo/doc/normativa/bed-and-breakfast/circolare-prot-pg-08-227543-del-3-10-2008/view
42 MutuiOnline S.p.A. http://www.mutuionline.it/
43 Trattoria da me - 1937. https://www.facebook.com/trattoriadame/
44 Da Bertino e figli. http://www.ristorantedabertino.it/
45 la Repubblica. pagina VII. martedì 23 giugno 1992.
46 Comune di Bologna. http://www.comune.bologna.it/comune/servizi/17:6117/6116/

Printed in Great Britain
by Amazon